The Fighting Rabbis

The Fighting Rabbis

Jewish Military Chaplains and American History

Albert Isaac Slomovitz

NEW YORK UNIVERSITY PRESS

New York and London

NEW YORK UNIVERSITY PRESS
New York and London

© 1999 by New York University
All rights reserved
First published in paperback in 2001.
Library of Congress Cataloging-in-Publication Data
Slomovitz, Albert Isaac.
The fighting rabbis : Jewish military chaplains and American
history / Albert Isaac Slomovitz.
p. cm.
Includes bibliographical references and index.
ISBN 0-8147-8098-9 (cloth)   ISBN 0-8147-9806-3 pbk.
1. Chaplains, Military—Judaism—History. 2. Chaplains,
Military—United States—History. 3. Rabbis—United
States—History. I. Title.
UH23.S56 1999
355.3'47'0973—ddc21   98-58003
                           CIP

Manufactured in the United States of America

10 9 8 7 6 5 4 3 2 1

Dedicated to my beautiful wife, Gail,
and our wonderful children,
Rachel, Aaron, Leah, and Ilana.

Contents

Preface

The mission involved danger, possibly death. The U.S. First Division expected to attack in the morning. The most likely battle area required a nighttime reconnaissance. Three officers led the patrol. Throughout the night they sent back messages by runners. Occasionally they came close to machine-gun battles. As dawn approached they returned, tired, muddy, and exhausted, having accomplished their goal of gathering invaluable information for the upcoming attack.

One of the officers in this First World War mission was the Seventy-seventh Division chaplain, Rabbi Elkan Voorsanger. For his participation in the patrol and for other acts of bravery and devotion to his soldiers, Chaplain Voorsanger received a number of medals. His troops named him "The Fighting Rabbi." The story of this fighting rabbi and hundreds of other Jewish chaplains like him is an unknown and untold saga in American-Jewish history.

In Irving Howe's social and cultural history of New York Jewry, *World of Our Fathers*, no reference is made to the new immigrants and their children who entered the military in relatively large numbers prior to the First World War. Moses Rischin's *The Promised City* meticulously details the search for community by first- and second-generation Jews in New York City. No mention, however, is made of the armed forces as a possible means of assimilation for a new American-Jewish community. Deborah D. Moore's focus on the second generation of New York City Jews in *At Home in America* suggests no linkage between the emerging values of a new generation and the notion of patriotism and service to the country that certainly existed. Other scholars, such as Naomi Cohen, who so extensively chronicled the early years of twentieth-century Jewish community growth, have not fully considered the concerns the Jewish community expressed for their co-religionists in the military.

The significance of this omission by major historians cannot be overstated. Most American Jews are unaware of the long tradition of military service to their country. There is an unfounded belief that, except at times of national emergency, Jews have not had a place in the armed forces. In fact, while many Jews are justifiably proud of Israeli military war heroes, they are oblivious of their own American-Jewish heroes, who also deserve recognition, study, and admiration.

This paucity of scholarship is not absolute. There have been some attempts made to record the history of Jews and their rabbis in the armed forces. Rabbi Bertram Korn, a rear admiral in the Naval reserves, wrote a scholarly record of Jews in the Civil War. One chapter dealt with the chaplaincy issues of the period. Other works about the Jewish chaplaincy have been written by former rabbis in uniform. Rabbis Lee Levinger and Louis Barish wrote and edited personal and anecdotal accounts of their experiences. The problem with the existing scholarship is that it is fragmented and not compiled in a systematic manner.

Similar difficulties have become apparent as other faith traditions have begun exploring their military histories. Recently, Father Donald Crosby authored *Battlefield Chaplains: Catholic Priests in World War II*, a book that offers anecdotal accounts of priests in the Second World War. Broader historical issues regarding Catholic service in the military have not yet been addressed.

This book seeks to remedy this situation within American-Jewish military history. First, it demonstrates the long-standing ties and concerns between the broader Jewish community and Jews in the military. For over three centuries, Jews have been actively articulating and pursuing their rights to participate in the defense of their country and to have military rabbis with them. The strength of this relationship has been reflected in the development and growth of the Jewish Welfare Board into the single agency responsible for the spiritual and welfare needs of all Jewish military members. The intrafaith composition and longevity of the organization make it unique in American-Jewish history.

A second area of consideration concerns anti-Semitism. When contemporary society was infused with anti-Semitism, the military functioned as an institutional force representing equity and religious sensitivity. This notion is contrary to what many American Jews think. They believe erroneously, in a view often expressed to me, that the armed forces represented yet another segment of American society tainted with anti-Semitism. The truth, borne out by numerous primary documents and countless personal experiences, indicates that exactly the opposite is the case. Throughout the history of this country, rabbis and their Christian colleagues, working together as military clergy, helped create a practical ecumenism that promoted interfaith understanding. These military chaplaincy experiences built a foundation for future interfaith programs in the larger society.

The final area of research describes the unique histories of military rabbis. Their motivations, training, religious services, counseling, battlefield experiences, sacrifices, and reflections need to be recorded, studied, and appreciated. The story of these rabbis in uniform helps refute the misperception that military service has not been embraced by Jews. This book confirms the facts. American Jews and their rabbis, from the country's earliest days, have had a full and participatory place in the defense of their country.

Lastly, the contemporary relationship between the larger Jewish community and Jews in the armed forces needs to be reassessed. Military Jews are rapidly becoming lost in the everchanging mix of issues and topics occupying the time and money of institutional and denominational Judaism. What started out as a tidal wave of concern for Jews in the military exactly one century ago has diminished to a mere trickle of consideration for contemporary Jews and their rabbis in the armed forces. This book is meant to help the wider Jewish community appreciate its past so it can better rearrange its priorities of the present.

Acknowledgments

The following institutions have graciously assisted in my research: the Jacob Rader Marcus Center of the American Jewish Archives, the American Jewish Historical Society, Jewish Welfare Board Jewish Chaplains Council, the National Archives, the Nimitz Library at the United States Naval Academy, and the U.S. Army Chaplain Museum. I am also grateful to the West Point Jewish Chapel Fund for providing a subvention to assist in the publication of this project.

Dr. Bill Galush gave scholarly direction and constant support. Mr. Edward Marshall, Ms. Barbara Breeden, and the late Father Thomas Hogan provided encouragement. Members of my immediate and extended families have been helpful and supportive from the beginning of my Ph.D. studies. I owe them special thanks.

To all those rabbis and chaplains who have preceded me, I offer my heartfelt gratitude. Your historical achievements ensured that the men and women of the United States armed forces were able to seek and find divine guidance in the midst of loneliness, personal challenges, battles, and war.

Many prayers were made in the course of this work. I feel it is appropriate to offer one at this time. Blessed are You, Lord our God, King of the Universe, who has given us life, sustained us, and permitted us to reach the occasion of this book's completion.

The Fighting Rabbis

1

The Genesis of the Chaplaincy

The story of Jewish chaplains is part of the larger history of military spiritual leaders. From Biblical times to our own, soldiers and sailors have wanted their endeavors blessed by holy men and women. The American military chaplaincy, on the eve of the Civil War, represented centuries of tradition regarding this unique ministry. In its evolution, the U.S. military came to represent a wide variety of religious and ethnic groups. The growth of the American-Jewish community in the years leading up to the Civil War prepared the way for the first U.S. military rabbis.

The Hebrew Bible vividly describes examples of holy men inspiring fighters to victory. In one instance, when Moses held up his staff on a mountaintop as a rallying symbol for the Israelites, they prevailed in battle against the Amalekites.[1] A second account, from the book of Deuteronomy, shows the connection between the priest and those fighting:

> Before you join the battle the priest shall come forward and address the troops. He shall say to them, Hear O Israel! You are about to join battle with your enemy. Let not your courage falter. Do not be in fear, or in panic or in dread of them. For it is the Lord your God who marches with you to do battle for you against your enemy.[2]

This inspirational relationship between the fighters and those blessing the battle developed and became the norm through much of subsequent history.

These spiritual guides eventually received the title of chaplain. This designation may be traced to a fourth-century Gallic legend concerning Saint Martin of Tours. During a military expedition, Martin offered half of his cloak to a freezing beggar. That same night, he had a religious vision that convinced him to abandon his military career for a life devoted to religious work. Eventually he became the patron saint of France. The remaining half of his cloak became a sacred relic and was utilized as a rallying symbol in battle by French kings. The word "chaplain" derived from the French "chapelain," which referred to the officer assigned to watch over the cloak.[3]

In the eighth century, various church councils and synods forbade clerics from taking up arms and participating in civil or military actions. This principle of clerical-military separation began to evolve at a time when priests and bishops functioned as land barons and defenders of their territories, often against fellow Christians. A church document from 803 detailed some of the ecclesiastical responsibilities of an early military chaplain. In addition to not shedding blood, clergy selected for military duty were expected to offer mass, hear confessions, impose penances, anoint the dying, and assist the wounded.[4]

As modern armies grew from smaller feudal forces, a permanent corps of military chaplains emerged. Alexander Farnese, duke of Parma in the late sixteenth century, organized an elaborate system of military clerics for Spanish forces. Farnese produced an army that included clerics as part of its organizational structure. A clergyman served with each company unit. The chaplaincy developed to such an extent that the Pope appointed a representative from the Holy See to function as a vicar-general of the Spanish army. In November 1587, Farnese endeavored to create a permanent corps of military chaplains. He petitioned the Society of Jesus, which provided him with twenty-four Jesuits. They founded a separate ministry that dealt exclusively with military personnel. Eventually, Jesuits also served as spiritual guides to the Spanish navy.

As the Jesuits established themselves in the Spanish military during the sixteenth century, similar developments occurred in the English armed forces. In the Royal Navy, as with most seagoing ventures, the crews desired a minister to solicit divine guidance with the hopes of a successful and safe voyage. The famous adventurer Sir Francis Drake, whose father was a naval chaplain, utilized the Bible as a means to rally his crew in dangerous situations. The religious and social benefits of having a chaplain on board were outlined in instructions associated with the Cadiz expedition that set sail in 1596, led by Admiral Charles Howard:

> That you are to take special care to serve God, by using of Common prayers twice a day. . . . You shall forbid swearing, brawling, dicing, and such disorders as may breed contention and disorders in your ships; wherein you shall avoid God's displeasure and win his favor.[5]

Having a chaplain present thus helped maintain the morale and fighting spirit of the crew.

Large scale English sea movements, such as the 1588 battle with the Spanish Armada, and subsequent journeys of exploration routinely included military ministers. The need for such men became so urgent that the English government raised special funds to ensure that the various ships in the fleet sailed with a seagoing chaplain.[6] Military clerics participated in the English armies as well. In the late seventeenth century, a description of the military clergy reflected the contemporary sense of ecumenism: "The preacher, be he priest or minister whether Lutheran or Reformed or Roman Catholic, his office is well enough known and there is much respect to be paid him. . . . His duty is to have 'care of souls,' and it is well if he meddle with no other business, but make that his only care."[7] This type of ecumenism became an integral part of the chaplaincy. Chaplains prayed for and worked with all those on their ships or in their units.

This English-style chaplaincy became part of the military structure in colonial America. Chaplains joined militia units and cared for the spiritual needs of the troops. In 1637, in one of the initial battles against Native Americans in the Pequot Wars, Reverend Samuel Stone accompanied colonial forces from Connecticut. A question of whether an attack should be initiated was referred to the chaplain for his prayer and endorsement. The success of the battle supported the minister's role as beseecher of divine guidance: "We had sufficient light from the Word of God for our proceedings."[8] Local ministers became chaplains in a variety of ways. Governors and legislatures appointed some clergy, while others were chosen by militia leaders or volunteered for service with a specific unit.

George Washington, as a colonel in the Virginia militia, noted the significance of the chaplaincy. In a series of letters sent to the Virginia legislature, Washington repeatedly asked that funds be allotted for a chaplain for his unit. He expressed the need for a spiritual leader in a letter dated September 23, 1756: "The want of a chaplain does, I humbly conceive, reflect dishonor upon the regiment. . . . The gentlemen of the corps are sensible of this and did propose to support one at their private expense. But I think it would have a more graceful appearance were he appointed as others have been."[9]

Washington's familiarity with and approval of chaplains continued throughout his career. In his various papers and correspondence, Washington made over fifty references to chaplains. This material reveals that Washington had four definite ideas about the functions of chaplains. The first involved the most traditional role. Chaplains interceded with Providence to secure protection and victory for the soldiers. Toward this goal each regiment was to procure the services of an outstanding chaplain, who prayed daily for the rights and liberties for which they fought.[10]

In a second role, chaplains symbolized the conscience of the army. They were to speak against drunkenness, gambling, and other activities that weakened the cohesiveness of the military unit. A third and extremely important activity of these spiritual leaders dealt with troop morale. At Valley Forge, during the difficult winter of 1778, military clerics worked arduously to improve the morale of the troops. This spiritual encouragement helped the men in their crucial decisions to persevere at their posts through the winter.

The fourth task of military clergy, as envisioned by Washington, was to increase unity and harmony among the troops. At the regimental level, chaplains administered to all troops; sermons derived from the Hebrew Bible (the Old Testament) were especially popular. Some of Washington's troops were Roman Catholic and Jewish. On one occasion, he circulated to his men a sermon written by a civilian rabbi. The future first president concluded that a unified army that allowed the free exercise of religion would serve as a model of tolerance for the new nation. By the time Washington assumed command of the Continental Army in August 1775, fifteen military clerics serving twenty-three regiments were in place. From 1771 to 1783, 179 ministers served under the revolutionary flag.[11]

Recognition of the importance of a military chaplaincy came in an early act of Congress. In March 1791, Congress authorized the president to establish a new army regiment. The act made a specific provision for a military chaplain. In that same month the Reverend John Hurt, an Episcopalian who had served extensively with the Continental army, became the first chaplain of the new republic's army.[12]

In the early decades of the nineteenth century, the army and navy had very few chaplains on active duty. These military ministers were some of the initial teachers at (the Military Academy at West Point and the Naval Academy at Annapolis.) One of the first chaplains at West Point, Thomas Picton, described his dual role of teacher and minister: "As a minister, my chief duty is to preach on Sundays; as teacher . . . I am trying to teach them World Geography, World History, Morality and Law among nations."[13] Naval chaplains participated in the movement to abolish the practice of flogging sailors and also participated in significant voyages. Chaplain Charles Stewart sailed on the USS *Vincennes* around the world in 1829–30. Naval chaplains accompanied Commodore Perry on his expeditions to Japan in the 1850s.[14]

On the western frontier, many traveling clergy became unofficial chaplains at isolated army posts. These pastors were so well received that the inhabitants of the posts wrote letters to Congress requesting that they be appointed as military clergy. In 1838 Congress passed a bill that allowed fifteen frontier installations to choose local clergy, who became salaried military chaplains. Their congregations included pioneer-settlers as well as Native Americans being exposed to Christianity for the first time.[15] By the 1840s, the navy and army had about two dozen active-duty chaplains.

As the chaplaincy grew, it evolved in terms of its denominational composition. At the time of the Mexican-American War, military clerics represented various Protestant groups. Mexican propagandists suggested that the United States Army wanted to deprive Mexicans of their Catholicism. To counter this accusation and to minister to the large number of Catholic soldiers, President James K. Polk requested from the Catholic bishops of New York and Saint Louis two priests for service with the army in Mexico. Father John McElroy and Father Anthony Rey volunteered for the assignment. Father McElroy served as a hospital chaplain, ministering to the wounded. He also organized a school for local children. Father Rey accompanied the troops as they went into battle; during an assault on Monterey, he distinguished himself in caring for the wounded. In a subsequent encounter with Mexican guerillas, Father Rey was killed. He was the first priest to die on active duty. Technically, Fathers McElroy and Rey were not official army chaplains, as the President did not have the legal authority to appoint them. Congress granted that authority to generals and the secretary of war. The first Catholics officially appointed to the army saw service in the Civil War. The navy appointed its first priest in the 1880s.[16]

Throughout the early 1800s, questions about the constitutionality of the military chaplaincy were occasionally raised. At the time of the Mexican-American War, a small movement arose that called for the abolishment of the military chaplaincy, based on the constitutional principle of the separation of church and state. In March 1850, the Judiciary Committee of the House of Representatives responded to a number of petitions it had received urging "that the office of chaplain in the army, navy, at West Point, at Indian stations, and in both houses of Congress be abolished."[17] The House's reply was that the constitution had expressly given Congress the authority to raise, support, and regulate an armed forces. The role and work of military chaplains were an integral part of that process. It also noted that chaplains had successfully served in the military from the time of the revolution and that "it was fully within the power of the Congress to provide for the appointment of chaplains as that of surgeons."[18]

While chaplains had their status confirmed, Jews followed another path to become part of the military chaplaincy. Since arriving in America, Jews have had an active role in the defense of the country. The first Jewish settlers came to America in 1654, arriving at the Dutch outpost of New Amsterdam. These pioneers had fled from the Dutch-controlled settlement of Recife in northern Brazil, which had been retaken in battle by the Portuguese. Part of their motivation for fleeing was a wish to avoid the Inquisition's sphere of authority by entering the New World. These Jewish refugees quickly began to assimilate into the larger colony. The governor, Peter Stuyvesant, sent a petition to his employers, the Dutch West India Company, recommending that the Jews be expelled. The Jewish group sent an opposing petition requesting to remain. They reminded the directors of the Company that "many of the Jewish nation are the principal shareholders of the Company."[19] Their petition to remain was granted.

This process of sending petitions to the main company in Holland became the procedure for attaining many of the privileges they desired. They requested and received the rights to build synagogues and own property. In August 1655, the Jewish refugees won the right to be part of the local militia and take on the responsibility to help protect their homes and colony.

Throughout colonial America, Jews of Sephardic (Spanish) and Ashkenazic (European) traditions built synagogues, cemeteries, and businesses. Most Jews supported the American revolution. Approximately one hundred Jews enlisted in the Continental army, half of them as officers.[20] The Declaration of Independence, the Constitution, and the Bill of Rights symbolized ideals that had been historically denied to Jews. America allowed Jews to practice their religion and to be loyal citizens. In August 1790, President George Washington, in responding to a letter from a Newport synagogue, reiterated this principle:

> All possess alike liberty of conscience and immunities of citizenship. It is now no more that toleration is spoken of, as if it was by the indulgence of one class of people, that another enjoyed the exercise of their inherent natural rights. . . . May the children of the stock of Abraham, who dwell in this land . . . sit in safety under his own vine and fig-tree, and there shall be none that make him afraid.[21]

These themes of liberty and constitutional guarantees of religious freedom became an integral part of America. Jews would not hesitate to fight for these rights.

In 1779 Thomas Jefferson introduced a bill that established religious freedoms for all Virginians. Passed into law in 1785, it became the standard for most other states. A few states, such as Maryland, instituted laws that required an allegiance to Christianity as a requirement for public office. Jews and their supporters argued against the unfairness and illegality of the Maryland law, and by 1825 it had been amended to allow other faith groups to pledge their allegiance to the state.[22]

During the early decades of the 1800s, German Jews, along with other Germans, Irish, and other ethnic groups, emigrated to America. Many Jews had experienced political and social discrimination in Germany. The aborted revolution of 1848 in Germany had also created uncertainties for Jews. For many, America beckoned as a land of possibilities. In the words of Leopold Kompert, eminent Czech-Jewish novelist, offered in 1848: "Our goal must, therefore, be emigration, the founding of a new fatherland, the immediate achievement of freedom."[23] Most of these newly arriving Jews came without savings. Many engaged in the profession of petty-tradesman, carrying goods on their backs throughout the small towns and rural districts across America. Over time this type of work often led its practitioners to owning a small store in a newly developing area in the heartland of America and to becoming financially secure.

German Jews formed their own social groups and clubs. The Independent Order of the B'nai Brith represented the largest of these organizations. Patterned after the Masons, B'nai Brith Lodges created secret passwords, initiations, and special titles for their leaders. Affiliation with such a lodge became a coveted social distinction for German-American Jews. Membership in these clubs exceeded the number of people who belonged to synagogues.[24]

Many German Jews, by the onset of the Civil War, enjoyed success and comfort. They opposed attempts to convert them and for the most part did not intermarry. The Jews of America were free, perhaps freer than Jews had been for centuries. America, with her never-ending frontiers, offered innumerable economic and religious opportunities.

On the eve of the Civil War, Jews knew that they would be called to fulfill their patriotic duties in the North or South. Up to this time, no rabbi had served as a Jewish military chaplain. With over one hundred and fifty thousand Jews in America, this would change, but not without a fight. In the spirit of the ancient Biblical leaders, Jews going to war wanted the blessings of their own holy men as they entered into battle and faced death. As we shall see, they succeeded eventually in getting them.

2

The First Military Rabbis
Fighting for Equality

Religion played a crucial role in the Civil War. The prevailing religious ideologies of the North and South performed significant functions in the context of the war, inspiring those on both sides. Within the armed forces, the prevalence or lack of clerics played a significant role. Initially, rabbis were prevented by law from becoming military chaplains. A broad-based community movement to amend this legislation took place in the first year of the war. The Jewish community pursued this issue on constitutional grounds and with confidence. It reasoned that Jewish men in battle had the right and need to have their rabbis with them.

Gardiner H. Shattuck has suggested that religious beliefs in the North and South contributed to the ultimate Union victory. In northern churches, spiritual leaders actively involved themselves in the war. Many believed that their role included the reforming of society toward a greater good. This belief in the righteousness of their cause was reflected in the fact that the number of revivals among Union forces increased as it became more apparent that the North would prevail. Southern religious ideology, on the other hand, emphasized the worth of the individual's moral development and theoretically resisted the notion of Christian participation in secular affairs.[1] Southern citizens therefore lacked similar encouragement from their spiritual leaders, a situation that may have affected morale.

While the chaplaincy became more effective in the North, in the South it never developed into a highly organized part of the armed forces. In fact, in its initial planning for a military structure, the Confederacy excluded any mention of a chaplaincy. After a few months without military clergy, the Confederate Congress, reacting to the protests of some ministers, authorized Jefferson Davis to assign chaplains to military regiments. Within a few months, the same Congress lowered the amount of pay that had been promised to these clergy. The Congress wanted to ensure that the clergy served as a religious calling, not for the money. As a result, many of the chaplains resigned their positions. By the spring of 1862, more than half of the Southern regiments lacked military clergy. The situation remained the same, with the exception of some work done by individual clerics, throughout the war.

Major church organizations such as the United States Sanitary Commission and the United States Christian Commission made substantial contributions to the Union war effort. The Sanitary Commission spent over twenty-five million dollars providing foodstuffs, blankets, clothing, and medical supplies for army medical and nursing units. The Christian Commission provided religious tracts, Bibles, and other reading materials for the troops. They enlisted thousands of volunteers, who worked with doctors and chaplains aiding and assisting the soldiers. Both of these organizations significantly enhanced the morale and spiritual welfare of the Union forces.[2]

While these commissions were important elements in the religious welfare of the troops, military chaplains lived and prayed with them on a daily basis. Chaplains came into the military with the hundreds of thousands of state militiamen and others who volunteered for service. In the North, the president and military leaders desired that spiritual mentors be made available to as many troops as possible.[3] General Orders Fifteen and Sixteen, issued by the War Department in 1861, reflected this desire for military clergy. These orders authorized regimental commanders who did not have clerics to appoint them. Officers of the regiment interviewed and selected potential candidates. In some cases, ministers enlisted in the regiment and then sought election to the chaplaincy. Quite often, this approach was successful, as the officers felt that they were selecting "one of their own." The only formal criteria concerning the minister were that he be approved by the particular state governor and be an ordained minister of some Christian denomination. Once these conditions were met, the cleric received a commission from the War Department.

The Christian focus of these criteria did not go unnoticed. Representative Clement Vallandigham of Ohio moved to amend the provisions of the orders regarding the chaplaincy requirements, proposing that the law be expanded to include rabbis. As Bertram Korn notes, Vallandigham's assertions came on his own initiative: "Without any Jewish prompting, he spoke out clearly in defense of Jewish rights."[4] The Congressman based his comments on the assertion that these regulations implied that the country was a Christian one, which had not been the intention of the founding fathers. The Ohioan's amendment did not engender much debate, nor did it pass. The bill became law in its original form, though the Christian requirement would later foster additional debate.

Military clergy had a number of responsibilities. Their primary task involved the organizing and conducting of religious services. Often, their sermons dealt with loyalty to the military and the reality of death in battle. In many regiments military clergy were the postmasters, delivering, collecting, and sorting all personal correspondence. Chaplains also counseled their troops about drinking and gambling, and listened to their troubles. Occasionally, military pastors volunteered to be the personal bankers of the soldiers. They carried thousands of dollars back to the hometowns and families of the men in their regiments. During the course of the war, over two thousand five hundred chaplains served Union forces, though no more than six hundred were on duty at any one time.[5]

As the war intensified, the number of wounded and casualties quickly grew. Permanent military hospitals began replacing the field hospitals that had provided initial care for the wounded. Diseases such as measles, typhoid, and malaria took their toll on the troops as well. In the midst of so much pain and suffering, the spiritual needs of the sick and dying went unfulfilled. The law provided for regimental clergy, not for hospital ministers. In July 1862, Congress passed legislation that allowed for the appointment of chaplains for permanent military hospitals by the president and the War Department. The daily responsibilities of these clergy included writing and mailing letters for

A relaxed scene in a Union camp, where counseling for all sorts of issues might have taken place. Courtesy National Archives, Civil War Collection.

sick soldiers, counseling them, conducting religious services, maintaining and organizing libraries, and providing other recreational activities to help speed their healing. During the war, over five hundred northern clergymen served in these positions.[6]

Jews and other minority groups naturally participated in the conflict as well. Jews in the North and South, for the most part, gave their allegiances to the areas in which they resided. Out of one hundred and fifty thousand Jews in the country, approximately six thousand five hundred served with Union forces, while two thousand joined the Confederacy.[7] Some regiments formed in the North came from predominantly Jewish neighborhoods. One such combat unit from the Philadelphia area, the Sixty-fifth Regiment of the Fifth Pennsylvania Cavalry, precipitated public debate when it chose a Jewish officer,

Michael Allen, as its spiritual leader. Allen, a native Philadelphian, took this position with a strong background in education and Judaica. He had studied Judaism with Reverend Isaac Leeser, a prominent American-Jewish preacher.[8] Although the choice of Allen seemed logical, it was illegal, as he was neither Christian nor ordained.

When he acted as the regimental chaplain, Allen's sermons considered the faiths and backgrounds of all his men, according to Bertram Korn: "Theologically, his sermons approached the various aspects of religion; immortality, ethics, faith from a common Judeo-Christian background. They were realistic, practical, down-to-earth talks, designed to touch the most basic problems of men stationed only a few miles from the battle-front: fear, restlessness, doubt, and homesickness."[9] He gave English lessons to the many new Americans in his regiment and functioned as an able minister to his troops. In September 1861, in response to reports of unworthy and ill-prepared clergy functioning as military chaplains, the Young Men's Christian Association (YMCA) visited and evaluated various camps. Their representative came to the Sixty-fifth Regiment and discovered Allen, its non-Christian, nonordained chaplain. This situation was put into a YMCA report about unfit military chaplains and generated a public outcry.

Within a few weeks, Allen resigned his commission with the regiment. In his resignation, he cited health concerns, but clearly the attention and notoriety of this case were motivations as well. The public discussion surrounding this incident became so widespread that Assistant Adjutant General of the Army George D. Ruggles published an official policy statement on the topic. This statement reiterated the requirements for a military chaplain: "Any person mustered into service as a chaplain, who is not a regularly ordained clergyman of a Christian denomination will be at once discharged without pay and allowance."[10]

The Sixty-fifth Regiment decided to create a test case of the legal requirements for a military chaplain. The regiment contacted Rabbi Arnold Fischel and requested that he become the regiment's new chaplain-designate. Fischel, who had a New York City congregation, immediately accepted the invitation. He seemed to be an ideal candidate for the position. In addition to his work as a civilian clergyman, Fischel

Captain Michael Allen. Courtesy Marcus Center, American Jewish Archives.

was a member of the Board of Delegates of the American Israelites, which involved work in Washington, D.C., as a lobbyist for Jewish causes. This board, formed in 1859, was comprised of twenty-five congregations and represented an early communal organization for Jews.[11]

Despite Rabbi Fischel's prominence in the Jewish and secular communities, Secretary of War Simon Cameron rejected his application to become a military clergyman. The basis for the denial revolved around the chaplaincy provisions that clearly called for clergy to be "of some Christian denomination." The publicity surrounding the rejection of Rabbi Fischel galvanized the Jewish community. Individuals and groups determined that this chaplaincy requirement must be changed. They utilized three complementary methods to achieve this goal: publicity, a petition campaign, and lobbying efforts.

Jewish periodicals reported extensively on this issue. The father-and-son editorial team of Samuel and Myer Isaacs wrote for the *Jewish Messenger*. They suggested that the chaplaincy provision recognized Christianity as the dominant American religion and reduced Judaism to the status of a second-class, inferior faith.[12] The Isaacs called on the Jewish community to clamor for a change in the law. They and other editors averred that equal treatment under the law was the preeminent issue in this case. They also proposed that all minority groups should have the chance to be represented in the armed forces. The Jewish community actively pursued what their ancestors had asked of Peter Stuyvesant two hundred years prior—equal opportunity to serve their country.

Support for this activist approach also came from the secular press. Metropolitan newspapers from New York, Philadelphia, and Baltimore offered editorials favoring equal representation for Jews under the chaplaincy provisions. The editor of the *Baltimore Clipper* reminded his readers that Congress itself had a rabbi open a legislative session with prayer: "How was it that the same body could deny Jewish soldiers the right to share the prayers of the same clergyman?"[13]

Opposition to their efforts surfaced from some Christian groups. Publications such as the *Presbyter* opposed the notion that non-Christians might be considered for the chaplaincy. Their concerns extended to "Jewish rabbis, Mormon debauchees, Chinese priests, and Indian conjurors."[14]

The second element of the campaign to modify the chaplaincy law involved the sending of letters or petitions to Congress and the president. Prominent community leaders such as Rabbi Isaac Mayer Wise, in his newspaper the *Israelite*, strongly supported the petition drive: "Wherever Israelites live draw up a petition to abolish that unconstitutional law, have it signed by every neighbor you find disposed to do so, and send it to your representative or senator in Congress."[15] Congress received hundreds of such petitions. Some came from individuals, while others, such as the one prepared by F. Friedenreich of Baltimore, contained the signatures of seven hundred Christians.[16] One typical letter used by Jews mentioned the inadequacy of the existing law and then argued that, under the Constitution, all religions should receive equal consideration. It then referred directly to the war:

> While many who profess our religion are fighting the battles of our country, exposed to all the hazards of war, the authorities are precluded from appointing even one chaplain who might from his position be enabled to afford religious consolation to such Israelites as may be dangerously wounded or found in a dying condition on the field of battle, or lying in the hospitals. . . . The subscribers therefore respectfully pray of your Honorable bodies that the words Christian ordained clergymen, or their equivalent, may be stricken out, and the various laws so altered without delay, as to afford to your memorialists that redress for which they justly ask.[17]

It is significant that this process took place against the backdrop of a country in the initial months of an uncertain war.

In addition to the extensive publicity and petition drives, the Board of Delegates of American Israelites formulated a third approach. The board requested that Rabbi Fischel himself lobby the president about the chaplaincy law. On December 11, 1861, Fischel, who utilized his political contacts to secure a visit, met briefly with the president. Lincoln read the documents that Fischel had brought with him and asked questions. He initially responded that the issue, although new to him, had merit. In a subsequent message to the rabbi, Lincoln wrote that he planned on recommending to Congress some changes in the law regarding the chaplaincy in general: "I shall try to have a new law broad enough to cover what is desired by you in behalf of the Israelites."[18]

The campaign to modify the chaplaincy regulation began in December 1861. By the summer of 1862, a clear consensus arose to amend the existing law. A proposal to modify the legislation underwent many revisions between the Senate and House versions and eventually became law. In July, Congress decided to add an additional clarification to the chaplaincy provision. This additional provision reinterpreted the prior requirement of "some Christian denomination" to read, "That no person shall be appointed a chaplain in the United States Army who is not a regularly ordained minister of some religious denomination."[19] Under this new interpretation, rabbis became eligible to serve as chaplains.

At this juncture, though the appointment of a rabbi to a predominantly Jewish regiment might have occurred, it did not. The first rabbis to enter the military did so as hospital chaplains. It is unclear why a rabbi did not immediately apply for a regimental chaplaincy position. Certainly there would have been only a few regiments like the Sixty-fifth that had a majority of Jewish men. Perhaps by this time, the rigors and horrors of war had become apparent and caused individuals to be reluctant to undertake such responsibilities.

As large military hospitals began to be built and staffed, as mentioned above, they required spiritual healers. Two rabbis joined with hundreds of other clergy in this new area of ministry. They were subject to military discipline and regulations, as were the regimental clerics. All hospital chaplains were commissioned by the president and War Department and came under the supervision of the surgeon general of the army, received assignments to hospitals in the cities of their residence and worked with hospital surgeons.[20] The first military rabbi, Jacob Frankel, was the fifty-four-year-old leader of Rodeph Shalom Congregation of Philadelphia. The Board of the Hebrew Congregations of Philadelphia nominated him to President Lincoln, who in September 1862 appointed him as a hospital chaplain.

Frankel had a musical background and spent much of his time entertaining sick and wounded troops. His position in the hospital was a part-time ministry; in addition to his hospital work, he maintained his community synagogue. During religious holidays, he arranged for the Jewish personnel to get furloughs so they could attend services in town. Local rabbis worked as volunteer chaplains at other hospitals and performed many of the same tasks as Frankel.

Bernhard Henry Gotthelf from Louisville, Kentucky, became the second rabbi appointed to the hospital ministry. He received his commission in May 1863 and served throughout the war. One of his accomplishments included the establishing of German language libraries in various military hospitals. Jewish and non-Jewish patients, more comfortable with German utilized these facilities. One local newspaper in promoting these libraries noted that there were thousands of sick and wounded German speaking patients in Louisville's military hospitals, including two to three hundred Jewish patients.[21] Gotthelf submitted monthly reports of his work to the Surgeon General, as did Frankel. These reports gave brief accounts of which hospitals they visited and their assessments of the general morale and also dealt with routine military matters.[22]

The third and final rabbi appointed as a military chaplain during the Civil War served as a regimental chaplain under somewhat unusual circumstances. Ferdinand Leopold Sarner arrived in America from Germany in 1859 as a thirty-nine-year-old rabbi with a doctorate in philosophy from the University of Hesse. He served as a congregational rabbi for one year in Rochester, New York. His next endeavors are unknown, but in April 1863 he became the chaplain of the Fifty-fourth New York Regiment, known as the Hiram Barney Rifles and the Schwarze Yaeger. In his initial interview with the regiment's officers for the position, Sarner presented a letter from the Prussian ambassador in Washington which reflected his academic degrees and evidence that he was an ordained clergyman. However, none of these documents specifically mentioned his rabbinic ordination. This regiment consisted primarily of non-Jewish German speakers with a few Jewish soldiers. It is possible that Sarner, seeking employment in a new country, took the

Some patients and caregivers in a Civil War military hospital, where hospital chaplains would have practiced their ministry. Courtesy National Archives, Civil War Collection.

opportunity to utilize his overall religious and particular German linguistic skills and signed on as a general chaplain rather than specifically as a rabbi in uniform.

It is unclear whether Rabbi Sarner fully represented the first regimental Jewish cleric. In fact, as Korn indicates, some military records listed him as an ordained minister of the Lutheran Church.[23] Alternatively, he may have served as a liberal Jewish chaplain, taking into account the various faith traditions in his regiment. While the regiment saw military action, Sarner's exact chaplaincy activities went unrecorded. In January 1864 he was wounded at Gettysburg. The serious nature of the injury generated a medical discharge from the service on October 3, 1864.[24]

Some of the men of Rabbi Sarner's Fifty-fourth Regiment prepare for battle.
Courtesy National Archives, Civil War Collection.

Evidence exists of civilian rabbis who fulfilled their patriotic responsibilities as well. One rabbi, Max del Banco of the Reform Congregation of Evansville, Indiana, died in a steamboat explosion while returning home from conducting High Holiday services for Union forces at
Vicksburg in 1864.[25] Rabbi Maxmilian J. Michelbacher from Beth Aha-
bah Congregation of Richmond, Virginia, wrote a special prayer for
Confederate soldiers, which he printed and distributed to as many men
as possible. Even a small portion of the prayer is still powerful: "Here
I stand now with many thousands of the sons of the South, to face the
foe, to drive him back, and to defend our natural rights. O Lord, God
of Israel, be with me in the hot season of the contending strife; protect
and bless me with health and courage to bear cheerfully the hardships
of war."[26]

In the absence of military rabbis, individual Jews tried to make contact with fellow Jews in civilian communities wherever and whenever possible. Colonel Marcus Spiegel, a Jewish officer of an Ohio regiment, wrote letters home that spoke of meeting coreligionists and attending holiday services with them in Norfolk, Virginia, in 1862.[27]

Regarding rabbis in the Confederacy, Bertram Korn maintained that no record exists of any formally appointed Jewish chaplain. Dr. Louis Ginsburg, a Jewish scholar, wrote to the American Jewish Archives that he possessed anecdotal evidence that a Reverend Uriah Feibelman had served as a Jewish chaplain with Confederate forces, yet no primary or secondary sources supported this assertion. Dr. Jacob Marcus, founder of the American Jewish Archives, suggested that perhaps Feibelman, along with other Jews, fulfilled their regular assignments and then functioned as religious lay leaders on a regular basis.[28] Given the relatively disorganized Confederate chaplaincy, this explanation seems the most likely one.

The service of Reverend Abraham D. Cohen, chaplain for the Forty-sixth Regular North Carolina Infantry, represented an unusual chaplaincy case. Cohen, born in England in 1822, was the regiment's Baptist chaplain. His letter of resignation, dated December 20, 1862, kept his specific faith undeterminable: "I have received an appointment from an association in Georgia to preach to the soldiers in Savannah. . . . Under the circumstances I think I could be more useful to the cause of God and country in this proffered position than the one I now occupy."[29] Cohen may have been a Baptist with a Jewish name or a new convert to the Baptist religion.

In addition to having Jewish chaplains in the military, albeit a very modest number, other minorities came into the armed forces. Catholics represented one such group; Catholic immigrants provided soldiers in significant numbers to the North and South. In most cases, they did not have access to a military priest. Archbishop John Ireland, who served as a chaplain with the Fifth Minnesota Infantry Regiment, wrote that the Catholic Church in America had neglected its soldiers: "Numberless thousands of Catholics scattered through the Army never saw a priest during the war. No one was near them at the moment of death. Provision should have been made to have a priest attached to each division."[30] Approximately forty priests served with Union forces, while the Confederacy utilized twenty-eight.[31] Some of these served with a regiment only for a brief period, then returned to their home parishes.

African Americans represented another minority culture brought into the military. By the conclusion of the war, over one hundred and eighty thousand black troops served in the Union army. The Union did not sanction African-American officers to lead these troops. This was done by white combat officers, who in turn elected their own chaplains. While white chaplains ministered to most of these regiments, black clergy served fourteen of them. Their work involved typical chaplaincy duties: preaching, counseling, engaging in educational activities, and dealing with the hardships of war. Henry M. Turner, pastor of the Israel African Methodist Episcopal Church in Washington, D.C., was appointed by President Lincoln in November 1863 as the first black chaplain.[32]

The inclusion of these minority faith groups within the military produced opportunities for cultural understanding, but attempts at inclusion were not always successful. The First Wisconsin Regiment of Heavy Artillery elected as their chaplain Mrs. Ella Hobart, a member of the Religio-Philosophical Society of Saint Charles, Illinois. After she had served for nine months, a recommendation for a commission was forwarded to the president. Lincoln responded: "The President has not legally anything to do with such a question, but has no objection to her appointment."[33] But Secretary of War Edwin M. Stanton disapproved her application to be a military cleric. He did not want to set any precedents altering the gender requirements of the chaplaincy. As a result, no female chaplains served during the war.[34]

While the war created some possibilities for increased ethnic and religious understanding, in some cases it helped reinforce previous stereotypes. As the war progressed, legal and illegal commerce between northern and southern traders occurred on a regular basis. During 1862, with the Union victories in the Mississippi Valley, the pace and volume of such trades increased dramatically. Northern businesses needed raw cotton, while salt, shoes, medicine, and gunpowder remained in short supply in the Confederacy. Many individuals, including high ranking officers from both sides, participated in this speculative and profitable commerce. According to one observer, Charles A. Dana from Memphis, in 1863, "Every colonel, captain, or quartermaster is in secret partnership with some operator in cotton; every soldier dreams of adding a bale of cotton to his monthly pay."[35] Union Generals Sherman and Grant attempted to terminate this illegal trade with a series of proclamations and military enforcement. These efforts were mostly unsuccessful, and the trade continued.

While most of these speculators were not Jewish, it was Jews who were singled out for punishment. Grant and other Union generals often complained about Jewish "speculators whose love of gain is greater than their love of country."[36] In December 1862, General Grant issued Order Number Eleven, which was drafted specifically against Jews: "The Jews, as a class, violating every regulation of trade established by the Treasury Department, and also Department Orders, are hereby expelled from the Department."[37] Jews living in the territory covered by Grant's order were forced to leave their homes and businesses. Within days, Jewish representatives contacted the president and requested that the order be rescinded. Lincoln agreed. He found it inappropriate, especially since it designated a whole group of people, thousands of whom had fought or were fighting for the Union.

Other anti-Jewish sentiments were expressed during the war. Korn indicates that northern newspapers routinely used the term "Jew" or "German-Jew" when referring to any Jewish individuals accused of disloyalty. In all areas of the captured Confederacy where illegal trade occurred, "Jews" received blame as the primary agents. One newspaper article about Jews concluded, "The people whose ancestors smuggled for eighteen centuries smuggle yet."[38]

The Confederacy reflected somewhat similar stereotypical views. Confederate Congressman Henry S. Foote of Tennessee claimed that Jews had flooded the country and controlled at least nine-tenths of the business of the land; "if the present state of things were to continue, the end of the war would probably find nearly all the property of the Confederacy in the hand of Jewish Shylocks."[39] An editorial in a Charleston, South Carolina, newspaper denounced people who made illegal profits. It then suggested that Jews as a class should not be singled out as the primary agents of this practice. The editorial's mention of this suggests that the refuted belief was widely held.[40]

These prejudices, expressed so openly, held enormous implications for subsequent Jewish-American history. John Higham suggests that such anti-Jewish incidents be considered within the context of other wartime prejudices. Yet he also described Grant's Order Number Eleven as "an act that may stand as the principal nativistic incident of the war years."[41] Naomi Cohen avers that later nineteenth-century American Jews singled out the Civil War years as the onset of serious anti-Semitism in the United States.[42]

Despite such forecasts, the situation for the Jews in the Civil War period was very positive. The fledgling Jewish community, with the substantial support of non-Jews, fought for the constitutional privilege of equality. The rapidity of the change in the chaplaincy provisions was especially significant when viewed within the backdrop of a civil war. Within a brief period, through the most democratic means of publicity, petitions, and lobbying, the law of the land was changed. Two rabbis served as military chaplains in hospitals, and Rabbi Sarner saw service as a regimental minister. Jews who were fighting for their country had won the privilege of having their own clergy enter the armed forces with them. This process of forcefully and publicly speaking up for their rights would be a recurring dimension of Jewish life in America.

3

Fighting Anti-Semitism

In the five decades that bridged the Civil War and the First World War, the attention and efforts of the Jewish community toward their coreligionists in the military expanded in a dramatic fashion. A number of reasons explain this heightened attention: an increase of anti-Semitism in America, which included the charge that Jews were unpatriotic and did not serve in the armed forces; the entrance into the military of a significant number of newly arriving immigrants, whose spiritual needs had to be met; and the increasing growth of Jewish communal organizations.

Following the Civil War, anti-Semitism in America became a more significant element in contemporary society. In June 1877, Joseph Seligman, a prominent Jewish American, and his family were denied admission into the Grand Hotel in Saratoga, New York. The hotel's owner, Judge Henry Hilton, left no doubt about his intentions: "Judge Hilton . . . has given instructions that no Israelites shall be permitted in the future to stop at this hotel."[1] While this incident did not receive universal approval, some accepted it as a precedent to be emulated. Austin Corbin, developer of Coney Island as a resort area, publicly supported Hilton's stance: "We do not like Jews as a class . . . they make themselves offensive to the kind of people who principally patronize our road and hotel."[2] Others suffered from this type of intolerance as well. In 1887, the anti-Catholic organization, the American Protective Association, came into existence. The goals of this group were direct and crass: "Never vote for a Catholic, never go out on strike with one, or hire a Catholic when a Protestant was available."[3]

The Jewish community did not have a clear consensus as to the origin of this anti-Semitism. Many Jews believed that it represented a continuation of the historic, stereotypical attitudes found in Europe. Others felt that Jewish success in America and acceptance into the middle class had created an environment of envy that brought about the prejudicial charges.[4] Sydney Ahlstrom suggests that Jews took on the role of scapegoats for a variety of society's ills: "City dwellers, peddlers, bankers, non-Protestants. . . . What is important after the 1880's is that the Jews are explicitly included in anti-foreign attacks, while previously this had rarely been the case."[5] The extent of the discrimination and its acceptance can be illustrated by the advertisements of some hotels and escorts: "No dogs. No Jews. No consumptives."[6]

This anti-Semitism took on a new form when the patriotism of Jews became an issue. In December 1891, a letter to the editor of the *North American Review* alleged two serious charges against American Jews:

> I had served in the field for about 18 months . . . and was quite familiar with several regiments. . . . I cannot remember meeting one Jew in uniform or hearing of any Jewish soldier. . . . I learned of no place where they stood shoulder to shoulder, except in General Sherman's department, and he promptly ordered them out of it for speculating in cotton and carrying information to the Confederates.[7]

This characterization of nonpatriotism was echoed by Mark Twain in an essay in which he stated that the Jew "is charged with a disinclination patriotically to stand by the flag as a soldier. By his make and his ways he is substantially a foreigner and even the angels dislike foreigners."[8] While in later years Twain retracted this statement, his earlier writings gave this prejudice wide acceptability.

Such biased comments received some credibility from academic sources. In 1891 Goldwin Smith, an historian at Cornell University, averred that Jews functioned as a closed group within American society. Jewish tribalism, he claimed, was set forth in the Old Testament (Hebrew Bible) and the Jewish Law Codes (Talmud). This tribalism prevented Jews from being patriotic to the countries in which they lived. Smith also wrote that Jews believed themselves to be a superior people whose ultimate goal included the domination of the world's economy.[9] Smith's views meshed with contemporary racist and nativist theories that classified new immigrants as inferior to those who had come earlier to America. He further asserted that Jews were incapable of being patriotic, as indicated by their willingness to constantly change countries rather than show allegiance to any particular one.[10] The general response by the Jewish community was to ignore or disparage such remarks. Some individuals did react to such accusations. Rabbi Edward Calisch wrote an essay praising the fighting spirit displayed by Confederate Jewish soldiers; Rabbi Max J. Kohler authored a series of articles entitled "Incidents Illustrative of American Jewish Patriotism."[11]

Simon Wolf, an activist and prominent representative in the Jewish community, chose to respond to these antipatriotic charges as well. Wolf devoted his life to Jewish and secular causes and organizations. He was involved with the Hebrew Sheltering and Immigrant Society, the Independent Order of the B'nai Brith, the Masons of the United States, and the Red Cross Association, and was instrumental in raising large sums of money to build asylums in Atlanta and Baltimore.[12] Various presidents appointed him to political and diplomatic positions. He devoted much time to the treatment that Jews received in Russia. Wolf's stature aided him in his quest to respond to the allegations of Jewish nonpatriotism.

In 1895 he published a three-hundred-page book listing, by state and family name, over eight thousand individuals whom he authenticated as having been Jewish who served in the Civil War. The book also contained written comments from senior officers praising the Jewish soldiers who had fought with them in various campaigns. His philosophy was simple: "that the Jew as an American citizen will take high rank in the history of our country, and will never prove recreant to its best tradition, and vindicate by his conduct his right to American citizenship, and transmit to generations unborn, his love of, and for, all that is humane and noble, and is ready in peace and in war, to battle for all that which is elevating and patriotic."[13] The publication of Wolf's book offering facts and figures about Jewish involvement in the armed forces helped refute prejudicial accusations.

This type of direct response to the charge of nonmilitary involvement was also reflected in the first edition of the *American Jewish Yearbook*, written in 1900. It listed by name and service affiliation Jews who had served in the Spanish-American War.[14] Also in response to the charge of nonparticipation in the Civil War, a new fraternal club was formed. In 1896, seventy-eight Jewish veterans of the Union army came together in New York City. The group, known today as the Jewish War Veterans, named itself the Hebrew Union Veterans Association of the Civil War. At their opening meeting, they pledged their allegiance to America and pledged to "combat the powers of bigotry wherever originating and whatever the target; to uphold the fair name of the Jew and fight his battles wherever unjustly assailed . . . to gather and preserve the records of patriotic service performed by men of Jewish faith; to honor the memories and shield from neglect the graves of Jewish heroic dead."[15]

As a result of the renewed debate about Jewish patriotism and the presence of a growing number of Jews in the military, the organized Jewish community began expressing its concerns. In September 1898, Rabbi H. Pereira Mendes, president of the Orthodox Jewish Congregational Union of America, sent a message to Major General Henry Corbin, the adjutant general of the army (the chief administrative officer for the War Department). This letter gave the dates of that year's High Holidays and mentioned the religious significance of these days. The note asked that Jewish soldiers be granted leaves of absence in order to reach their homes in time for the holidays. A direct response came within three days: "I have the honor to state . . . furloughs will be granted to soldiers of your religious faith, making application therefor, to celebrate the holidays set forth and instructions will be given accordingly."[16] Other Jewish organizations became involved in similar communications.

In 1899 the Union of American Hebrew Congregations, represented by Simon Wolf, sent a comparable request to the adjutant general's office concerning the upcoming Passover holidays. This message included information about prayer services and special Passover food requirements. General Corbin specified that not only would local commanding officers grant holiday leave, but that they would also "allow them facilities for partaking of such food as prescribed by the religion."[17] This decision allowed individual commanders to give approvals based on the unique circumstances of their command.

This practice of Jewish organizations informing the War Department of upcoming Jewish holidays and religious needs continued on an annual basis. In response to a 1902 letter from Dr. Mendes, the adjutant general reflected a familiarity with the prohibition for Jews against eating leavened bread during Passover. The general offered his department's assistance in an unusual endeavor, agreeing to transport unleavened bread (matzoh) from San Francisco to a base in Manila in time for the Passover holiday.[18] By August 1904, President Theodore Roosevelt, after receiving correspondence from various community leaders, also became involved. He issued executive orders to the War Department about the upcoming High Holidays. The president also directed that Simon Wolf and the Reverend H. Mendes be apprised of his actions.

A number of factors may have been included in the president's involvement. Acting upon a request from community leaders represented sound politics. However, receiving holiday accommodations may also have been an increasingly important issue for Jewish military personnel. A growing Jewish military presence required that commanders be familiar with Jewish holidays and dietary needs. Also, individuals such as Wolf may have used this topic to illustrate to the president the growing number of Jews in the armed forces. Eventually, messages concerning Jewish holidays and special religious needs became part of the military's normal, annual administrative process.

In addition to religious organizations communicating about Jews in the military, Jewish newspapers became involved. In February 1902, the publishers of the *Jewish Daily News* wrote to Secretary of War Elihu Root. The letter mentioned that year's approaching Passover holiday. The editor expressed an unusual motivation for his letter: "We have been requested by a large number of enlisted men of the Jewish faith to write to you on their behalf and to tell you of their desire to be permitted to participate in the religious services in the eating of unleavened bread which is the feature of the Jewish Passover."[19] This request received the same response as the others; commanding officers could grant leaves of absence as needed for Jewish personnel.

This concern for Jews in the military was soon articulated by political figures. In January 1904, New York City Congressman William Sulzer from the Fifty-fourth District requested that the War Department supply him with a count of Jews in the military and the number of chaplains and religious faiths represented in the chaplaincy. Secretary of War Elihu Root replied that his department had no means to ascertain the number of any faith group within the armed forces. Root also reported that, of the fifty-seven chaplains serving, none were Jewish.[20]

In May of that year, Congressman Henry Meyer Goldfoggle from the Fifty-seventh District of New York City requested from the adjutant general's office the number of Jewish personnel who requested leaves of absence to observe Passover and other religious holidays. The army responded that it had no means of gathering such information. However, the adjutant general informed his post commanders that they should become familiar with this issue in case such information might be requested in the future.[21]

As the presence of Jews in the armed forces increased, the question of rabbis in uniform to meet their religious needs once again surfaced. Despite an expansion of the Chaplain Corps, the practice of replacing a retired or deceased clergy with someone of the same denomination made entries by different groups very difficult. In December 1908 a new Jewish fraternal association, the Federation of Jewish Organizations of New York State, addressed the subject of rabbis as military chaplains.[22] The goals of the federation were "to promote the material, intellectual and moral welfare of Jews and to secure for Jews equal rights all over the world and to repel attacks against the Jew because he is a Jew."[23]

The group initiated two major resolutions. The first dealt with the Russian government's treatment of American Jews visiting and offering assistance to impoverished Jewish villages in the Pale of Settlement. The second concerned itself with the lack of rabbis in the armed forces. A preamble to the resolution noted that the government maintained chaplains of various religious denominations to meet the religious needs of soldiers and sailors, and yet no rabbis served in the military. The resolution called for Jewish organizations to petition Congress, the president, and the secretaries of war and navy to establish a chaplaincy position "for the religious comfort of Jewish citizens enlisted in the Army and Navy of the United States."[24]

Various political leaders received this resolution. A number of congressmen and senators supported the petition and promised to follow the issue closely. Congressman William Sulzer informed the federation that he had introduced a bill in Congress creating additional chaplain positions, some of which would be filled by rabbis. In a speech given to the federation in February 1909, Sulzer elaborated on his bill. First, he contended that a considerable number of Jews served in the military. While acknowledging that there was no accurate count of the number of Jews in the armed forces, he stated: "In war and in peace, on land and on sea, they [Jewish soldiers and sailors] do their duty faithfully, efficiently and courageously."[25] Sulzer concluded that these Jewish personnel required rabbis to meet their spiritual needs. He made clear his intentions: "This resolution of mine provides for three additional chaplains; They should all be Jews. Of course we cannot say that in the resolution. I have been trying to get it passed, but have not been able so far to do so."[26] Despite his efforts, this bill would not become law until the First World War.

The American-Jewish press reflected the community's interest in the military. In October 1908 the *American Israelite* featured a large picture on its front page showing at least a hundred Jewish personnel from Fort Leavenworth, Kansas, participating in that year's Passover meal.[27] This same paper, in its February 1910 edition, carried an article on the career of Admiral Adolf Marix, a Jewish naval officer. The story emphasized Jewish participation in the armed forces: "Many of the 5,000 Jewish soldiers and sailors who participated in the successful efforts to liberate Cuba from Spanish control (thus refuting the ancient and often repeated libel that Jews will not fight for their country) have just celebrated their tenth reunion in New York."[28]

In June 1911 the *Hebrew Standard*, a newspaper that represented the Orthodox community in New York City, editorialized about President

Taft's disciplinary action against an army officer who made disparaging remarks about Jews. The Anglo-Jewish newspapers focused on two concerns. First, the prejudicial view that Jews did not serve had to be refuted. Second, the needs of the growing Jewish military population had to be met.[29] The War Department, in a March 1911 response to the calls for military rabbis, contended that the number of Jews in the army was small and scattered throughout many posts. The department suggested that a Jewish chaplain would not have an effective ministry. Not addressed was the idea of a "roving rabbi," who would travel to different bases offering rabbinic coverage.[30]

By 1912 the efforts of the Jewish community on behalf of their coreligionists in the military and the need for rabbis in service intensified. In March, the Federation of Jewish Organizations created a new entity, the Patriotic League of America. The group patterned itself after other service agencies, such as the Young Men's Christian Association, that offered spiritual and religious assistance to their military members. Jewish personnel required a similar effort and organization. This new group advocated lofty goals: "To encourage patriotism, help Jewish soldiers and sailors fulfill their religious obligations, bring together Jewish military communities with near-by civilian rabbis and help get jobs for discharged veterans."[31]

Within a short time, news about this new group spread throughout the country. In January 1913, the Patriotic League issued appeals to rabbis asking that rabbis open their synagogues and temples to Jewish military personnel for the upcoming Passover holiday observances: "If we cannot all of us take our part in the ranks of the Army, the Navy and the National Guard, let us at least do what we can in befriending those who are already in the service of the flag."[32] The publicity generated much support. By the next year, a separate committee concerned with Passover observances for armed forces personnel formed as a new group under the auspices of the Patriotic League.[33]

On April 25, 1912, the House Committee on Military Affairs devoted a session to the question of rabbis in the armed forces. Those called to testify included Nissim Behar, the president of the Federation of Jewish Organizations of New York; Aaron W. Levy, an executive board member of the federation; as well as Rabbi Nathan Krass from

Temple Israel in Brooklyn, New York. In Rabbi Krass's testimony, he suggested that there were over one thousand Jews serving in the army without the benefit of Jewish clergy. In the question and answer period after his opening statement, he made two further points: first, that there were army forts in the New York area, such as Forts Slocum and Hamilton, that had hundreds of Jewish soldiers and where a rabbi could serve; second, that rabbis could easily minister to others: "Now there is absolutely nothing that a rabbi could, in a moral or religious sense, teach that could be in any way conflicting with the religious tenets of the Christian."[34]

In his testimony Levy spoke of the many letters that the federation had received from Jewish soldiers, which stated that while other faith groups had their clergy available to them, they did not: "The Jewish boys felt that they were left out because they had no one to whom they could appeal and no one to whom they were bound by close ties."[35] Nissim Behar summed up the group's motivations regarding contemporary prejudices:

> We want to show that the Jew fights; because it has been said even in churches that the Jew does not fight. And we know that the Jew is a patriotic citizen and we want to prove it. And we want to prove that we have our fair proportion of Jewish boys in the Army and Navy. It is also a question of principle which is just in harmony with the freedom from discrimination guaranteed by the American Constitution.[36]

From Congressional testimony to organizational commitments, the Jewish community's concern for their coreligionists in the military was active and substantial.

Major Jewish groups, such as the Young Men's Hebrew and Kindred Associations (YMHKA), the Jewish equivalent to the YMCA, became very involved in Jewish military issues. The YMHKA offered Passover and other holiday meals for Jewish personnel. It also sent Jewish social workers to various military camps to assist the men with social, recreational, and spiritual matters. By November 1914, Lewis Landes, the executive secretary of the Army and Navy Department of the YMHKA, wrote in the *American Israelite* that a substantial number of Jews served in the military. He estimated that there were ten to fifteen thousand Jews in the military out of a total force of one hundred and twenty-five thousand. He could not vouch for the accuracy of his figures, which he based on interviews held with Jewish personnel in at army forts and naval stations.[37]

Within the military, Jews dealt with the social phenomenon of anti-Semitism. In 1915, Major Le Roy Eltingle, an army instructor at Fort Leavenworth, Kansas, wrote a book entitled *The Psychology of War*. This textbook detailed the attitudes of various ethnic groups toward war. He used it to teach a course on warfare. The Jew did not fare well, in Eltingle's opinion: "He doesn't know what patriotism means. Recruiting officers find that he does not average up with other applicants physically. . . . The soldier's lot is hard physical work. This the Jew despises. He does not have the qualities of a good soldier."[38] The *Chicago Sentinel* republished these characterizations and wrote President Woodrow Wilson requesting an explanation. Within days, the War Department responded. The army informed Eltingle: "That the policy of the department is uniformly to discourage in the Army anything calculated to reflect in any manner on men of any particular race or creed and not to tolerate anything that would savor of race discrimination."[39] Eltingle received orders to review his book and expunge all the offensive portions.

Also in 1915, Congressman Walter N. Chandler of the Nineteenth District of New York City addressed a letter to the adjutant general. Chandler wrote that some of his Jewish constituents believed that Jews did not receive equal acceptances to the Military Academy at West Point or the Naval Academy at Annapolis. He further suggested that even if a Jewish person received an appointment to attend these academies, they anticipated discrimination and ostracism. The superintendent of West Point responded directly to these concerns: "No consideration of any kind is given at West Point regarding religious faith or belief of any candidate for the Academy. . . . In my more than ten years of personal connection with the academy I have never observed or heard of a case of social ostracism at West Point because a cadet was a Jew or of any other religious faith."[40]

This same correspondence reported that an 1899 investigation into the hazing of Jewish cadets turned up no such incidents. Also included

A band for entertainment at a Young Men's Hebrew Association army recreational facility, circa 1914. Courtesy Jewish Welfare Board Archives.

are letters of personal testimonies from men of the Jewish faith who had attended West Point and had not experienced any discrimination. Whatever the actual experiences of Jews at West Point may have been, there was a vivid contrast between the military's handling of questions of anti-Semitism and that of contemporary society. In April 1913, in Atlanta, Georgia, the Leo Frank incident occurred. Frank, an engineer, was hired in 1907 to be the plant superintendent in his uncle's company. He was accused of murdering a fourteen-year-old female employee of the company. Throughout the trial, Frank's Jewish background was raised. An anti-Semitic campaign repeatedly demanded the execution of "the filthy, perverted Jew of New York."[41] In August 1915, Frank, whose execution had been commuted to life in prison by Governor John Slayton of Georgia, was dragged from his jail cell and lynched.

While this type of social hatred and bigotry existed, it was officially unacceptable within the confines of the military. The primary task of the U.S. armed forces has been to create an effective fighting organization. By the very nature of our nation's beginnings, these forces have been composed of a variety of ethnic groups, with the exception of African-Americans who were fully integrated into the military in 1948. It was the task of the military to mold men of diverse backgrounds, languages, and beliefs into a single unit. At the core of this esprit de corps was the notion of mutual respect and awareness. To fight and to defend one another, troops required a basic creed of honor and integrity, a creed toward which Americans have always aspired. Troop morale and cooperation required mutual respect, not lynching.

As mentioned above, the Jewish community attached great importance to the task of ascertaining an accurate number of Jews serving in the armed forces. The project of obtaining accurate figures was undertaken by the Statistics Bureau of the American Jewish Committee in conjunction with the YMHKA. An article written by Lewis Landes for the 1916 *American Jewish Yearbook* reviewed their procedures and findings. Commanders in the army and navy received written questionnaires requesting the names of the Jews in their commands. Notices were placed on bulletin boards in barracks and on ships requesting that Jewish men send in their names and posts to a certain address to be counted. This methodology left some data uncounted. In some instances, the request was not received. In other cases, the men did not see the notices or the questionnaire or chose not to respond. Some Jews might have preferred to keep their religious affiliation private or might not have wanted to be identified solely on a religious basis.[42]

Nonetheless, out of 757 questionnaires sent, over three hundred elicited responses. The findings presented significant results. The statisticians concluded that while Jews represented about two percent of the overall population, they numbered approximately six percent of the military population.[43] These data suggest that a large number of first-generation Jewish men served in the military.

The fact that so many first-generation Jews entered the military was even more striking in light of the negative experiences that the Czarist army had held for Jews. Under the rule of Nicholas the First (1825–50), Jewish boys at the age of twelve were forcibly taken from their families for an initial period of six years of indoctrination, followed by an army career of twenty-five years. Communities had to fulfill quotas for conscription; if the numbers were unmet, communal agents known as *khappers* went among the villages, hunting for young children to kidnap and send to the army.[44] If these men survived the twenty-five-year period of service, their religious heritage rarely did. Similarly, in the 1880s, the May Laws promulgated under Czar Alexander III brought more upheaval for Jews. Every aspect of Jewish social, economic, and religious life was adversely affected. Jews were quickly driven into poverty. Organized pogroms, such as the one in Kishinev in April 1903, further humiliated the Jews and hastened their departure to America.[45] Yet for a variety of reasons—economic, social, personal, and patriotic—these same Jews joined the U.S. military and served with pride.

The desire to join the military may have been viewed as the ultimate form of Americanization. The author's grandmother, born in 1902, recalls that as a teenager, she and her contemporaries prided themselves on speaking English without an accent. They extolled their assimilation into a new culture. Certainly joining the armed forces provided one definite way of proving one's allegiance and affinity for a new homeland.[46]

In 1915 further examples occurred of the Jewish community's ongoing support and actions on behalf of its military members. That summer, individual rabbis attempted once again to join the service, and Jewish organizations recruited civilian rabbis to provide rabbinic coverage for the troops. In July 1915, Rabbi Julian Shapo of Tampa, Florida, sent an application to the secretary of war to receive an appointment as an army chaplain. He expressed compelling reasons for joining:

> Contemplating the considerable number of the Jewish faith already attached to, and now enrolling for service with the forces of our National defense and inasmuch as the religious wants of the soldiers of our creed have not received the spiritual benefits which entitles him, by reason of service in the Army to be equal with other denominations. I have concluded to offer my services.[47]

Rabbi Shapo did not enter the chaplaincy; his request was probably denied by the army. His descriptions, however, of the needs of the Jewish soldiers and sailors prompted various organizations to send civilian rabbis to minister to Jewish personnel while Congress considered a bill that contained provisions for additional (Jewish) chaplains.

The extent of the Jewish community's commitment became apparent in the summer of 1916, when three different organizations began providing civilian rabbinic coverage to Jewish soldiers. A large number of U.S. troops arrived in Mexico under the command of General John J. Pershing. These troops included a substantial number of Jews. Initially, the local branch of the Army and Navy Department of the YMHKA met the spiritual needs of these men. This group, based in the military forts along the Texas-Mexico border, sent social workers into the base camps to make arrangements for Jewish personnel to get time off for the upcoming High Holidays. Local rabbis and rabbinical students sent to the area conducted these services.

The Department of Synagog and School Extension Branch of the Union of American Hebrew Congregations also worked with the soldiers. When contacted by Rabbi Isaac Landman, corresponding secretary of the Central Conference of American Rabbis (CCAR), about its work with soldiers, the school extension responded:

> We are already engaged in religious work among Jewish soldiers on the Mexico front. Rabbi Samuel Marks has given up his vacation to devote himself to the religious and general welfare of the Jewish soldiers in the regular army of the National Guard in his territory. At his request we have sent copies of the leaflet reprints of the Union Prayer Book.[48]

A letter from Rabbi Marks indicated that the presence of the CCAR would be welcome, as the religious needs of the Jewish soldiers spread out in many bases were quite extensive.

Dr. William Rosenau, president of the CCAR, initiated a plan to further meet the needs of Jewish military personnel. He sent the treasurer of the CCAR, Rabbi Abram Simon, to meet with Secretary of War Newton D. Baker. In that meeting it was determined that there were at least two thousand Jewish men serving in the Mexico-Texas border area needing rabbinic coverage. The secretary proposed that perhaps a rabbi could function as a "detached chaplain," ministering to Jewish personnel in different regiments. Baker further recommended to Rabbi Simon that as soon as the CCAR appointed a rabbi for this mission, he would be provided with "an official order giving . . . every possible courtesy and attention, but no pay."[49]

Within one week, the CCAR decided that Rabbi Landman would proceed to the Texas-Mexico border to conduct holiday services and to function, as much as possible, as a military Jewish chaplain. The CCAR also sent out letters requesting contributions to a special fund to reprint prayer books for soldiers and to cover any expenses that Rabbi Landman incurred. In a letter addressed to Mr. Jacob Schiff, a prominent American-Jewish community leader, Dr. Rosenau indicated that a permanent Jewish chaplain could be appointed as soon as Congress passed and the president signed a new armed forces bill. The president, however, vetoed the bill that contained the provision for new chaplains.

Within days of his arrival, Rabbi Landman functioned as the coordinating agent for all Jewish activities. With the cooperation of the YMHKA and the Synagog Extension group, he canvassed the civilian and military communities and arranged High Holiday places of worship, obtained liturgical items, and ensured the issuance of prayer books. Landman's clearance from the secretary of war afforded him access to military information and the chain of command. Once he had determined the locations of the various regiments, he created a schedule of holiday services. For each camp Landman coordinated efforts with local synagogues or YMHKAs to host Jewish soldiers. For more isolated camps, he arranged furloughs and transportation to larger cities with existing houses of worship or sent a rabbi or rabbinical student to the camp to officiate. Some towns, such as Laredo, Texas, functioned as central meeting points for isolated troops. As noted by Landman, "By order of Brigadier General Mann, men of the Jewish faith at 31 outpost stations . . . were transported to Laredo for (holiday) services in army motor trucks."[50]

In a description of his holiday services, Landman portrays a fascinating view of services offered in a battlefield setting. During one service, 150 Jewish men prayed while 500 of their non-Jewish comrades surrounded them and respectfully followed along with the prayers. For the Jewish New Year service, Landman, assisted by Rabbi Lewis Landes, rose at 5:00 a.m. to prepare his pulpit, a ration-wagon made into a temporary altar:

> Not a single star as far as I had a record of them after the service out of the evening before, had disappeared. Out of the darkness and from all directions, men sprung up. Some of them were equipped for the march. These were from the Illinois and Wisconsin Infantry. They had to walk two miles through the night to reach Hill B, and back to join their companies after the services on the road. There we sat around the wagon, our numbers being constantly augmented, silent, thrilled with the moment and the occasion, waiting for the sun to rise. Soon the stars began to fade. A gleam of pink showed in the East. The barrels of a gun or two glittered, for a second, in the first rays of daylight. "Rabbi, the sun is rising," said one of the men. Never did that title mean more to me than at that moment. "The sunshine of the New Year," exclaimed another, "May God Bless Us." Silently, I climbed into the wagon and faced the rising sun. The men rose in their places, to the clank of their arms and accouterments and brought out their precious little prayer books. For my part, I was choked with emotion. I could not begin to read. "Bugler!" I said, trembling, to Bugler Sam Mehon of the Second Illinois Field Hospital, whom, the night before I had taught the sounds of the Shofar. "Bugler! Sound the Shofar!" and contrary to all traditions, I began a Rosh Hashanah (New Year) service with the sound of the Shofar. The long steady T'kiah call [long sustained sounding of the horn] served to have awakened the sun, to hurry in his course for the sake of these military men who were waiting to worship God, for, when I opened my book, I could read.[51]

Wherever he went, Landman received good-willed cooperation from military personnel. Because of his work and the participation of local and national Jewish organizations, hundreds of Jewish personnel worshiped and observed the holidays. In many ways, the work that Landman performed and the subsequent positive publicity that he generated served as a precursor to the work of rabbis in the coming world war.

On the eve of America's entry into the First World War, the Jewish community's relationship with its coreligionists in the military was quite substantial. There were a number of factors creating this strong alliance. As a response to social anti-Semitism and specifically the charge of Jewish nonpatriotism, individuals such as Simon Wolf, Jewish fraternal groups, and others reacted against this allegation. Significant resources were expended to ascertain an accurate number of Jews in the military, finding that a large number of Jews, many first-generation, were on active duty.

Most of the religious communities, the Anglo-Jewish press, and even new groups such as the Federation of Jewish Organizations of New York State, all actively represented the interests of Jews in the military to the War Department. Politicians, including Congressman Sulzer, responded to their calls for additional chaplaincy positions, which would include rabbis, by introducing bills in Congress. The community's support was also demonstrated in very tangible ways, as different religious groups provided rabbis and prayer books for soldiers serving with General Pershing. This interest and support by the entire community, previously unacknowledged by scholars, set the stage for subsequent developments at the National Jewish Welfare Board and the participation of rabbis in the coming war.

4

Rabbis in the Trenches

When America entered the First World War, the Jewish community's efforts to gain rabbinic representation in the armed forces came to fruition. The creation, growth, and subsequent work of the National Jewish Welfare Board represented the community's dedication to Jews in the military. In this war, twenty-five rabbis served on active duty. They were the first large group of rabbis to enter the armed forces chaplaincy in the history of America. Rabbis such as Elkan Voorsanger and Lee Levinger became pioneers in this field. Their ministries, and the manner in which they were integrated into the military structure, set a model for future generations.

When the First World War began in Europe in 1914, the United States hoped to maintain a stance of neutrality. However, by early 1917, most Americans realized that diplomacy had not achieved any substantial change in Germany's war policy. In April, Congress declared war and voted a massive conscription of men to fight. By June 1917 over 9.5 million men between the ages of twenty-one and thirty-one registered to serve their country. The total number of those who fought reached almost five million.[1] As part of this national call to arms, all citizens, including new immigrants, rallied to their nation's need. The War Department and other governmental agencies actively recruited immigrants for military and industrial service. These new Americans responded with a distinguished record of both service and support of the war.[2]

Within days of the declaration of war, the Jewish community met to organize its resources. The supervising council of the YMHKA determined that its organization did not have the capability to provide for the large numbers of Jews entering the military. They decided that the entire community needed to be involved in the effort to address the servicemen's religious needs.

On April 9, 1917, at the invitation of the YMHKA, representatives from seven major Jewish organizations came to New York City to devise a national approach to serving Jews in the military. This new advisory group was comprised of the Union of American Hebrew Congregations, the Central Conference of American Rabbis, the United Synagogue of America, the Council of Young Men's Hebrew Congregations, the Union of Orthodox Congregations, Agudas ha-Rabbonim (the Federation of Orthodox Rabbis), and the Jewish Publication Society. These organizations created the Jewish Board for Welfare Work in the United States Army and Navy. In March 1918 the name was changed to the Jewish Welfare Board (JWB).[3]

Other organizations desired to join the effort of these seven groups. Within one year, an executive committee representing various American-Jewish communal societies became part of an expanded administrative board. Other groups joining the JWB included the Independent Order of B'nai Brith, the Council of Jewish Women, the National Federation of Temple Youth, and the Women's League of the United Synagogue.[4] This board created a single agency that eventually included one hundred Jewish organizations that dealt exclusively with providing spiritual and material support for Jewish military individuals. The composition, subsequent achievements, and longevity of the JWB were unique. Previous attempts to galvanize the Jewish community across its wide-ranging spectrum of religious and social beliefs had not succeeded. In 1908 one attempt to unify the community in the areas of fundraising, religious education, and crime-fighting had some success in an entity known as the *Kehillah*. However, after six years the organization rapidly declined.[5]

In September 1917, the Commission on Training Camps, a governmental agency, recognized the JWB as "the official agency for Jewish welfare work in the military camps of the United States."[6] Both the Jewish community and the government, through a liberty-bond campaign, raised significant sums of money to fund programs initiated by the JWB.

The amounts raised for these efforts were impressive. By September

1918, the Joint Distribution Committee paid a lump sum of one million dollars to the JWB to fund its activities. This money had been raised through a series of Jewish Relief Campaigns held throughout the country. After this distribution, the JWB participated in a United War Work Campaign, created by President Woodrow Wilson to organize the seven major welfare agencies into one fundraising unit. This joint venture exemplified the philosophy of cooperation for the betterment of the troops; the JWB's portion was four million dollars.[7]

The success of the Jewish Welfare Board was due in part to its leadership. Prominent personalities, such as Dr. Cyrus Adler, associated themselves with the JWB and its mission. Adler brought enormous prestige and community contacts to his position as executive director of the JWB. He had a major role in the founding of the American Jewish Historical Society, as well as in that of the Jewish Publication Society. As a community organizer and an institution builder, he became a driving force behind the growing influence and status of the Conservative movement and the Jewish Theological Seminary.[8]

Another factor in the board's success was its ability to involve most of the organized Jewish community in its operations. Community branches were formed that included 165 Jewish communities in the United States, England, and France. Each branch, depending on its proximity to a military camp, organized committees on religious activities and personal services. The Committee for Religious Activities insured that Jewish servicemen were invited to religious services for all Jewish holidays. The Committee for Personal Services organized visits to military hospitals and distributed writing paper and literature to the soldiers. Batches of cookies and other treats were also distributed to the men.[9] Additionally, the JWB, in coordination with the Independent Order of B'nai Brith, jointly sponsored community centers in many larger cities. The purpose of these centers was to provide dances, lectures, and musicals for the benefit of military men.

As the board came together, communal organizations developed to serve soldiers of other faiths. According to Sydney Ahlstrom, at the onset of the war no civilian agencies, with the exception of the YMCA, ministered to Protestant service members. In May 1917, the Federal Council of the Churches of Christ in America initiated a meeting with

Star of David women handing out treats to military men during World War One. Courtesy Marcus Center, American Jewish Archives.

representatives from thirty-five Protestant denominations. This meeting resulted in the creation of the General War Time Commission. The primary goals of this group were to supervise activities and to provide for the religious needs of Protestant military men.[10]

Similarly, in August 1917, the Catholic church in America initiated the Committee on War Activities, later known as the National Catholic War Council. This organization coordinated the efforts of sixty-eight dioceses, twenty-seven national organizations, and the national Catholic press.[11] The association also supervised the recruiting and training of over a thousand priests. Additionally, the Vatican created the position of military ordinariate (bishop). This bishop became the source of pastoral care and religious authority for all Catholic priests and Catholics in the military.[12]

Structurally, the goals and programs of the three religious coordinating groups paralleled one another. They produced activities that covered a number of areas: recruiting and training denominational chaplains, supplying religious items for service personnel, training civilians for work at military bases, and building recreational facilities for troop entertainment. Often, the various groups' representatives worked together and shared common recreational facilities. In one instance, Rabbi Jacob Singer, assigned to Fort Riley, Kansas, conducted Jewish services in the Knight's of Columbus Welfare Hut, as the JWB had not erected its own building. On Sunday mornings he volunteered to play piano for the Protestant services.[13] In one of its first reports, the JWB acknowledged the cooperation of these groups. The report continued with an explicit statement of interfaith relations that foretold the inter-religious cooperation that ensued throughout the war.

> The idea is, indeed, to assist the Jewish youth in such a manner as shall enable him most readily to harmonize with the conditions surrounding him, to fraternize with his non-Jewish comrades, to have a better understanding of the point of view of those of other beliefs, and in turn to enable the non-Jew to have a better understanding of him.[14]

This spirit of cooperation applied to intra-Jewish relations as well. Even in areas of liturgical differences, the Jewish movements worked in an environment of teamwork and compromise. One of the first tasks undertaken by the JWB was the issuing of a standard Jewish prayer book. A committee of rabbis representing the three major movements in Judaism, Orthodox, Conservative, and Reform, came together and quickly created an eclectic prayer book containing a range of services, from Reform to traditional, from which the member could pray. This type of cooperation would remain a unique characteristic of the JWB throughout its history. Coordination with the Jewish Publication Society of America allowed the board to distribute 220,000 prayer books; 12 million pieces of JWB stationery; 6 million envelopes; thousands of ritual prayer objects, such as *talitot* (prayer shawls), tefillin (phylacteries), and mezuzot (ritual objects containing parchments with Biblical verses); and 185,000 Hebrew Bibles bound in khaki cloth. Additionally, Yiddish and Russian translations of government pamphlets on allotments, insurance, health, and hygiene were disseminated, along with Jewish songbooks containing Hebrew, English, and Yiddish songs.[15]

The ultimate mission of the Jewish Welfare Board was to meet the religious requirements of Jewish armed forces personnel. Three significant projects were undertaken to make it possible to accomplish this goal: the building of recreational facilities at military installations, the training of JWB civilian field-workers, and the recruitment of active-duty rabbis (and the supplying of religious and comfort materials to those rabbis). Initially, the JWB had utilized spaces in buildings already erected by groups such as the YMCA. To meet the increased need for space, the JWB constructed fifty new buildings at stateside and overseas bases. The programs that they organized for troops included dances, evening entertainment, social observances for Jewish festivals, English instruction for new immigrant soldiers, discussion groups, and access to JWB reading materials.[16] Additionally, for rabbis and welfare workers overseas, automobiles, typewriters, and other equipment was purchased and sent to JWB offices abroad.[17]

JWB field-workers coordinated the use of the buildings and developed many of the programs. They became known as the Star of David men and women. These individuals, like their counterparts in the Knights of Columbus or the Young Men's Christian Association, represented their denomination on a particular base or station. In the absence of a military rabbi, they also functioned as spiritual leaders and counselors for the Jewish troops. Training to become a field-worker for the JWB included an intensive, two-month period of instruction. The first month of vocational and educational training included lectures about religious perspectives on warfare, overcoming loneliness, draft laws, and the work of other welfare agencies.

The second month of fieldwork involved trainees in learning how to do a variety of practical activities: conducting Jewish services, designing social and entertainment programs, addressing issues of personal hygiene, and doing administrative tasks concerning the ordering and distribution of religious supplies.[18] By the end of the war, over three hundred people had served as JWB field-workers. These individuals brought impressive credentials to their jobs: "ninety percent were able to read Hebrew; more than half could read, write, and speak Yiddish."[19] They made an impressive and very significant contribution to the morale of the troops. When a base had a Jewish chaplain, these "Star of David" men and women worked with the rabbi in creating programs for the soldiers. The few active-duty rabbis greatly needed and welcomed the support of these field-workers.

Civilian rabbis became some of the first welfare workers. They functioned as auxiliary rabbis at camps and bases. A few ultimately entered service as Jewish chaplains. Others devoted a few months per year to serving the troops, then returned to their civilian ministries. The Knights of Columbus followed a similar process with the creation of a corps of auxiliary priests. These priests did not enter the military, but instead worked at various bases. They cooperated with active-duty priests, and in the absence of a military Catholic chaplain, they led services. Furthermore, local priests made special efforts to meet the religious needs of the Catholic troops stationed in their parishes.[20]

In addition to constructing buildings and training field-workers, the JWB began recruiting rabbis for the military. This task proved difficult, as no new chaplaincy spaces were available in the military ranks. The JWB and other Jewish groups renewed their efforts to create additional chaplaincy positions for military rabbis. In October 1917, five months after America's entry into the war, Congress proposed a bill that called for twenty additional chaplaincy positions. These chaplains would have the rank of lieutenant, earn $2,000 per year, and serve only during the war emergency. Congressional members understood that, although the proposed bill did not specify any religious denomination, groups such as Jews would benefit from its passage. The bill passed in a matter of days and went into effect immediately. Representative Isaac Siegel of New York City gave credit for the bill's passage to the Jewish Welfare Board, B'nai Brith, and other Jewish communal groups.[21]

The importance of the JWB was reinforced by the War Department. It wanted a central agency to represent the various organizations of American Judaism, through which all issues relating to Jewish chaplains and personnel would be answered. The Jewish Welfare Board, with its unique communal and rabbinic composition, met this need.

In fact, no appointment as a Jewish chaplain was allowed for any rabbi unless he had first received the recommendation of the Committee of Chaplains of the JWB.[22]

When the United States entered the war, a few rabbis immediately enlisted in the army. Until the bill allowing additional chaplains became law in October 1917, they served in the enlisted ranks and fulfilled their rabbinic roles as lay leaders. With the passage of the bill, the Jewish Welfare Board made a nationwide appeal to rabbis and their congregations:

> Nothing can be more important than that those who are charged with the performance of this sacred duty shall be men of character, tactfulness and intelligence, men who understand the soul of the Jewish boy and who can keep alive in the hearts of our youth the divine spark of our ancient faith . . . the services of rabbis are imperatively demanded.[23]

This plea also asked that congregations whose rabbis volunteered for service be willing to compensate their rabbis for the disparity between their military and civilian salaries.

As the JWB issued an appeal for rabbis, so did the Catholic Military Ordinariate. Various bishops and heads of religious communities received requests to release priests to serve in the military. Bishop Hayes, in charge of this effort, was direct in his appeal: "Were we not to provide chaplains and provide generously, for sons, husbands and brothers who have gone forth to battle, leaving behind at home sorrowing mothers, wives and sisters, the Church in America would be weighed in the balance and found wanting."[24] As these priests and rabbis entered the armed forces ministry, they, along with their Protestant contemporaries, made a significant contribution to the war effort.

Military chaplains played a highly visible and crucial role in the war. A 1917 book written for new chaplains by Orville J. Nave, a veteran chaplain, discussed their many responsibilities. In addition to describing the traditional roles of conducting services and providing religious education, Nave wrote specifically about battle conditions. He recommended that, once fighting began, chaplains be in the trenches encouraging their men. When wounded troops arrived at a field hospital, clergymen were to offer comfort and to function as medics:

> The chaplain must provide himself amply on the eve of battle with first aid supplies . . . including a hypodermic syringe, and such stimulants as the surgeon may think best, to be used with men whom the surgeon cannot reach . . . he must load himself with canteens of water and a suitable drinking vessel with a spout for men who must not be moved or cannot hold their heads up.[25]

This type of first aid was often lifesaving; words and prayers of encouragement also supported the healing process. Chaplains also assisted soldiers by helping with correspondence, providing items for recreation, maintaining a sense of hope, and offering solace. Nave's book also addressed the military minister's role in the recovery of the dead and severely wounded and the proper military rituals for use when conducting burial ceremonies.

In addition to the duties listed above, Jewish chaplains performed other unique tasks. Thousands of Jews who had volunteered for service were new immigrants, and they requested that their rabbis teach them about the English language, American history, and the U.S. government. Military rabbis also taught traditional Jewish study groups about prayers and Jewish ethics, and led discussions about contemporary issues. The discussion topics of one group held in Burgundy, France, included "Zionism and the Future of the Jew," "the Future Function of the Synagogue," and "Reconstructionism and the Returning Jewish Soldier."[26]

The assimilation of the rabbis into the armed forces chaplaincy and their accomplishments symbolized the cordial relationships enjoyed by Jews and Christians on many levels. Organizationally and individually, the mood of American soldiers during the war reflected themes of brotherhood and mutual respect. The experiences of Rabbi Elkan Voorsanger illustrated this phenomenon. In May 1917, Rabbi Voorsanger enlisted as a private with an army hospital unit. The bill creating the extra chaplaincy positions had not yet become law. Voorsanger had done volunteer chaplain work with troops assigned to General Pershing

Jewish Welfare Board Divisional Personnel at French Hospital. Courtesy
Jewish Welfare Board Archives.

in Mexico. His personal beliefs reflected a mixture of pacifism and
patriotism: "I am entering this war to register my protest against war.
. . . I can do that in no better way than to go to the front to alleviate
the suffering to those who know not why they go."[27]

In a letter to his family about the abruptness of his decision to
enlist, he noted that he did not want to claim any ministerial exemp-
tion from his duty to his country. He also reiterated his adherence to
his dual ideals of being antiwar and procountry. Within a few months,
Private Voorsanger had received his training as a medic and been trans-
ferred overseas for duty. By June 1917 he had earned a promotion to
sergeant. With the passage of the law for additional military chaplains
in October 1917, Sergeant Voorsanger received discharge papers as an
enlisted man and obtained reassignment as a chaplain with the rank of
first lieutenant with the American Expeditionary Forces (AEF). He
immediately began work as a chaplain. By December he had made a
number of recommendations to his commanding officer concerning

mail delivery for overseas troops. In February 1918 he was ordered to report to Base Hospital Number One for duty.

Voorsanger was one of the first military rabbis in the AEF, and the demand for his rabbinic services grew quickly. His enlistment and subsequent transfer to an active unit placed him months ahead of those rabbis who had waited for Congress to pass the bill opening up additional chaplaincy positions. His area of responsibility included large numbers of troops and widely separated bases. Jewish lay leaders and JWB workers came under his supervision as well. Voorsanger became the main point of contact for Jewish activities with French Jewish officials and other welfare agencies. He communicated his need for more rabbis and welfare items directly to the JWB.

In March 1918, the director of the YMCA in Paris wrote to Voorsanger requesting that he conduct a Passover meal (seder) observance. The YMCA covered all the expenses, including transportation and room reservations for Jewish soldiers. After the event, Voorsanger praised the organization: "How this war is breaking down prejudice, hatred and petty narrowness is indicated by such incidents as this—a Christian organization promoting a Jewish religious service and offering to foot the bill."[28] This type of interfaith awareness became a part of his extensive ministry.

Chaplain Voorsanger served as a pioneer for future Jewish chaplains. He ably fulfilled his specific rabbinic responsibilities and general chaplaincy roles without any difficulties or controversy. The military noted his many efforts on behalf of his troops. In June 1918 he received a promotion to senior chaplain of the Seventy-seventh Infantry Division. This advancement significantly increased his areas of responsibility. Voorsanger now supervised other military chaplains and represented the chaplaincy department in meetings with other senior officers. In the very brief history of the Jewish chaplaincy, no other rabbi had occupied such a prominent position.

Chaplain Voorsanger did not hesitate to meet the challenges of battle and war. After the Battle of Argonne, he received the Purple Heart for bravery. He was awarded the Croix de Guerre and was recommended for the army's Distinguished Service Medal. These accomplishments earned him the title of "The Fighting Rabbi." His

High Holiday services for Jews of the American Expeditionary Forces held in Young Men's Christian Association hut led by Rabbi Jacob Kohn in Chaumont, France. Courtesy Jewish Welfare Board Archives.

troops knew him as a chaplain who often put himself in the line of fire to minister to the wounded and dying. His earlier training as a medic helped him be useful in those situations.[29]

In October 1918, Rabbi Benjamin Friedman was ordered to the Seventy-seventh division. His arrival allowed Chaplain Voorsanger to focus more of his time of his supervisory responsibilities. Voorsanger reflected the strain of being the sole Jewish chaplain in his division when he greeted Friedman with the words, "Why are you so late in getting here?"[30] Out of the approximately 250,000 Jews who served, each rabbi was responsible for ten thousand. The ratio for other chaplains was about one per two thousand. Of the twenty-four Army rabbis and one Navy rabbi who came on active duty during the war, twelve served in overseas positions. Some of the rabbis in overseas locations arrived a few months before the war's conclusion. Nine other rabbis had been approved for the chaplaincy, but did not come on active duty due to the war's end. One rabbi, Harry S. Davidowitz of the Seventy-eighth Division, was severely wounded by shrapnel and, after many months of hospitalization, returned to America.[31]

Interestingly, the career of another chaplain, Rabbi Harry Richmond, somewhat paralleled Voorsanger's. Richmond, like Voorsanger, espoused pacifist causes. He enlisted as a medic, became a chaplain, and served in France. After the war, he returned to the civilian rabbinate, and was called upon in 1941 for the Second World War. Three other rabbis, Nathan E. Barasch, Julius A. Leibert, and Abraham Nowak joined Rabbi Richmond by having the distinction of serving in both world wars. Chaplain Richmond was the only one to have served overseas in both wars.[32]

Burial records of the Seventy-seventh division indicate that Voorsanger officiated at the largest number of military burials in his area. As the senior chaplain, his presence and prayers of committal added dignity to the military honors. He also became responsible for recording and collecting the personal effects of German soldiers buried by American personnel. Voorsanger wrote about this spirit of collegiality among the various chaplains. "In France there were no distinctions. The Fighting Rabbi says, A Chaplain was a Chaplain, not a Jewish Chaplain, a Catholic Chaplain or a Protestant. Each chaplain was responsible for the religion of every man, and it didn't matter to us how a man prayed, but that he prayed."[33] In February 1919, Chaplain Voorsanger resigned from the active-duty chaplaincy and became the JWB's director of overseas operations. His career, while somewhat unique, reflected the ability of rabbis to function simultaneously as Jewish chaplains and as spiritual leaders to all personnel. Other rabbis had similar experiences.

In 1922 Rabbi Lee J. Levinger wrote a book about his war-time duties entitled *A Jewish Chaplain in France*. In the opening pages of this book he expressed his thoughts about the role of military rabbis:

> He was first of all a Chaplain in the United States Army and second a representative of his own religious body. That means that all welfare work or personal service was rendered equally to men of any faith. . . .

Rabbi Chaplain Israel Bettan *(left)*, standing next to Rabbi Chaplain Elkan Voorsanger. Courtesy Marcus Center, American Jewish Archives.

Wherever I went I was called upon by Jew and non-Jew alike, for in the service most men took their troubles to the nearest chaplain irrespective of his religion.[34]

This attitude captured the contemporary thinking of the rabbis. They functioned as rabbis and chaplains to all.

Levinger's war experiences bore out this approach. As a chaplain in the 108th infantry, he worked in a field hospital unit, offering first aid and counseling to gas victims. Later, in October 1918, he joined a number of other military clerics, who had the sad task of searching deserted battlefields for unburied dead soldiers. They gathered personal items and sent them home. Final prayers for the dead were offered in an environment of interfaith sensitivity and respect: "We gathered together at the cemetery with a large flag spread out in the middle of the plot. I read a brief Jewish service, followed by Chaplains Bagby and Stewart in the Protestant and Father Kelly in the Catholic burial service, and at the end the bugle sounded taps for all those men of different faiths lying there together."[35] This attitude of mutual respect appeared regularly throughout the war.

The British Royal Army also exhibited religious sensitivity. It had nine rabbis, who worked arduously to visit all their military camps, hospitals, and training areas. In an account of his Royal Army chaplaincy service, Rabbi Michael Adler described some of his unique wartime initiatives. At his suggestion, a standard grave marker of a *magen David* (Star of David) bearing the word shalom was placed on the graves of all English, German, and later American soldiers who were Jewish, helping ensure that memorial prayers and permanent grave markers would accurately reflect their faith. For the Jewish New Year of 1916, Adler arranged for his services in France to be held in various cinemas, which his troops quickly dubbed "cinema-gogues."[36]

Jewish chaplains worked with the German forces as well, as Jews fought on both sides of the conflict. Thirty rabbis worked with the Prussian War Ministry on a contract basis and performed the same duties as their American counterparts. Their responsibilities as field rabbis included conducting services, making hospital visits, conducting funerals, and distributing religious literature and gifts from home. On

Stars of David and crosses on newly dug graves in an American military cemetery in Europe, World War One. Courtesy Jewish Welfare Board Archives.

the eastern front, at the request of the German high command, they coordinated relief activities for the Jewish civilian population in the war zone.[37] Rabbi Jacob Sonderling wrote of his experiences as a chaplain with the German army. During the war he conducted a seder in which Russian prisoners of war participated. They were counted as fellow Jews, not prisoners.[38] Reverend O. Nieduer, a German Protestant division chaplain, wrote a fascinating account of interfaith cooperation. "The Jewish Preacher," he wrote, "told me how he gave a service to a Protestant Army unit, how he let them sing the Lutheran hymn, how he preached about God who has helped us all and in whom we have confidence. . . . He prayed for the people and the country, for the loved ones at home, for the troops in the trenches, and the wounded in the hospitals. At the end they all sang, We stand before God the Just. I shook his hand. Mister Comrade, I wouldn't have done it otherwise."[39] How paradoxical that, in the midst of a world war, this type of cooperation existed!

This collegial attitude demonstrated itself in very pragmatic ways. The standard insignia for military clergy was the Latin Cross. In January 1918, Congressman Isaac Siegel from New York City forwarded a request to the army from the JWB that rabbis in uniform be permitted to wear some other insignia in place of the cross. Within two weeks of receiving this memorandum, the army issued the following directive: "Objection having been made to Jewish Chaplains wearing the prescribed insignia, you are authorized by the Secretary of War to omit the prescribed insignia."[40] Almost immediately, the quartermaster of the army solicited new designs for a Jewish chaplain's insignia.

Reports from the battlefront mentioned the difficulties of identifying rabbis without their insignia. An initial design suggested by the JWB recommended a six-pointed star (the Star of David). The army rejected this proposal, as the star appeared too similar to the stars worn by generals. Other designs included a seven-branched candlestick (menorah), a shepherd's crook, two lions of Judah supporting a Shield of David, and the tablets of the Ten Commandments surmounted with the Star of David.[41]

By June 1918, the issue had taken an interesting turn. General Henry Jerver, acting assistant chief of staff, suggested that all chaplains change their insignia back to that used prior to 1898—a shepherd's crook. He saw this return to an earlier insignia as a way of having a universal chaplain's device. Within weeks this became official policy. This policy drew a negative response from many Christian chaplains. In August General Pershing sent a cable to the War Department noting that his chaplains opposed the change.[42] Some Christian clergy felt that the change was appropriate: "I am a chaplain of the Christian faith, but I welcome the change. The shepherd's crook is symbolic of the chaplain's work."[43]

Once again the army reviewed the issues and considered three alternatives. First, that all chaplains be ordered to wear the same devices. Second, that rabbis be permitted to omit their insignia, and third, that rabbis wear a separate device that showed the Ten Commandments topped with the Star of David. In a short time, the third option became standard army practice. This process occurred while rabbis such as Voorsanger and Levinger performed their battlefield duties. It did not in any manner affect their ministries.

While the rabbis in the army received a satisfactory response to the insignia question, the lone rabbi in the navy did not have the issue resolved as quickly. Rabbi David Goldberg entered the navy in 1917. After his basic training, he was assigned to duty on the USS *President Grant*. Prior to reporting to the ship, he asked a senior navy chaplain about the propriety of a rabbi wearing the Chaplain Corps insignia of the Latin cross. The chaplain responded that the men understood that he wore the insignia of the corps and not of his faith group. A member of the JWB advised Goldberg to take his ship assignment and let the JWB deal with the insignia issue.

His experiences aboard the ship led him to request a transfer to a shore position. Out of six hundred men on the ship, only five practiced Judaism. Goldberg felt that the single chaplaincy position should be held by a Christian chaplain. As part of his ministry, he held services and developed educational and recreational activities. Nevertheless, he had intense misgivings about his ultimate effectiveness:

> The difference between a Christian minister and a Jewish Rabbi, in the deep-rooted belief of the men, is so vast and fundamental, that it leaves me almost beyond the pale, and while in the Submarine zone, in the sick bay, or at the death bed, I find that the men are left without spiritual consolation, as my own spiritual potency is almost nil.[44]

Goldberg continued with the process to get a transfer off the ship when he arrived back from deployment.

One of the differences between Goldberg's experience on the ship and those of his rabbinic colleagues in the army may have been caused by their contrasting situations. The army rabbis were literally in the trenches with their men; in these circumstances, a religious affinity might be more important than a specific denominational stance. On the ship, Goldberg's sailors may have felt these religious differences more acutely. Also, ship-board duty entailed an isolation from other Jews that the army rabbis did not face; they covered large geographical areas to be in contact with their men.

When Goldberg returned stateside, he received a number of letters from rabbinic colleagues who found fault with him for wearing the cross. He responded that the JWB should handle this issue and that, as a commissioned officer, he wore the cross as part of his official uniform. Nonetheless, by May 1918, he petitioned the navy to be allowed to wear the Star of David in place of the cross. His request pointed out that the army had dealt with and resolved the same issue. His request was denied. The navy felt that the Star of David was too similar to the insignia worn by admirals and solicited other options.

Goldberg then recommended that the Chaplain Corps wear the shepherd's crook as a universal symbol for all chaplains. This elicited, as it had in the army, some strong responses from Christian chaplains, including Goldberg's senior chaplain, John Frazier: "The Chaplain Corps of the Navy is more than satisfied to wear the Cross, and everyone of us who profess the Christian faith would resent most bitterly any effort to substitute any other insignia in place of the Cross."[45] Within a month, the navy authorized Chaplain Goldberg to wear the shepherd's crook.

Goldberg finished his two-year tour at Great Lakes Naval Base near Chicago, Illinois. During this tour, he edited a small book about chaplains on the base. Additionally, he spent much time carrying out rabbinic responsibilities. At one time there were over 2,600 Jewish personnel at the base.[46] After the completion of his two years of service, Goldberg continued his naval career as a reservist. He wore the shepherd's crook as his insignia until the Second World War, when the navy followed the army's example and allowed rabbis to wear the tablets and Star of David insignia.

With the end of the war, Goldberg and most of the rabbis quickly returned to civilian jobs. Some, such as Chaplains Voorsanger and Levinger, took positions with Jewish welfare agencies. They and their colleagues should be remembered as pioneers. A group of twenty-five rabbis entered the military and served their coreligionists and other service personnel in an atmosphere of mutual respect and cooperation. Indeed, Rabbi Voorsanger became a senior chaplain in charge of Catholic and Protestant clergy without a hint that anyone found this improper or unusual. A military system based on merit operated at its highest level. As a result of supporting these rabbinic pioneers, the rapid growth and development of the National Jewish Welfare Board, with its sense of intra-Jewish cooperation, became an historic model of communal cooperation and unified mission. It succeeded in meeting many of the recreational, emotional, and spiritual needs of military Jews.

5

The Interwar Years

The years between the two world wars saw a marked increase in anti-Semitism. This society-wide prejudice caused lost employment opportunities, produced publicly printed and broadcast stereotypical attacks, and legitimized groups that advocated Nazism. Yet the United States military, through its Chaplain Corps, symbolized one institution that stood against anti-Semitic beliefs. The armed forces clergy symbolized and practiced the ideals of mutual respect and equality. The Jewish Welfare Board and individual rabbis embodied the Jewish presence within these corps.

With the cessation of the First World War, the armed forces began a rapid process of demobilization. In the summer of 1919, over 2.5 million enlisted men and officers were discharged. By January 1, 1920, both the army and the navy were back to prewar levels of personnel.[1] As the military shrank, so did the chaplaincy. During the war there were over two thousand army chaplains; by 1922 this number had dropped to one hundred and twenty. The navy's corps of chaplains dropped by half, from two hundred to one hundred.[2]

Following the war, the government took over responsibility for the buildings constructed by the various welfare agencies. The JWB donated over twenty-five buildings to army and navy commands, salvaging equipment from additional facilities. Despite this transfer of tangible property, the board decided that the JWB retained a role in the military. A July 1919 resolution expressed this policy: "It was unanimously agreed that wherever there is an active camp . . . regardless of the small number of men of the Jewish faith in any camp or post, that activities of the Board should continue on the principle that the Board functions to all men."[3]

At this time the Board estimated that there were over five thousand Jewish men in the armed forces. These men were stationed at isolated bases and ships throughout the world, making the task of supplying them with Jewish objects even more difficult. Toward that end, the JWB supplied military posts with prayer books, Bibles, and Jewish literature. It also established and supported a lay leader system, where Jewish military men acted as liaisons between the board and post commanders. This system was particularly important due to the lack of active-duty rabbis. The JWB supervised or conducted services in 160 army posts, naval stations, military hospitals, and sanatoria. Despite the smaller number of soldiers and sailors, new military chapels were built in Honolulu, the Philippines, and the Panama Canal Zone.[4]

The board also looked after the over one thousand Jewish veterans in military hospitals. It provided volunteers and staff members to initiate visits, conduct religious and social services, and organize entertainment, all to assist in the recuperation of Jewish and non-Jewish veterans. The board also dealt with specific veteran's concerns, such as disability claims, insurance issues, and individual medical and financial needs.

Another major role the JWB played concerned military graves and the registration process. During the war, due to a lack of known religious affiliation and the need to rapidly bury soldiers, many Jewish soldiers had been buried in graves marked not with a Star of David, but with a cross. To remedy this situation, the JWB, beginning in early 1919 in France and continuing in Washington, worked with the American Red Cross and the Cemeterial Division of the War Department to examine every record of a wounded, dead, or missing soldier. Almost a half a million records were reconciled with information about Jewish soldiers killed in battle received from family members, relatives, friends, synagogues, and Jewish centers.

Once the identity of a soldier had been positively established, the Cemeterial Division verified the type of head-marker that was furnished for his resting place in a military cemetery maintained overseas. When inaccurate grave markers were corrected by the board, photographs of the properly marked graves were taken and sent back to relatives in America. This picture allowed grieving relatives back home to know that their Jewish soldier would always be correctly identified. Some of the fallen soldiers were brought back to the United States for burial in Jewish cemeteries. In such cases, the JWB helped arrange for a military escort and a rabbi to officiate at the burial service.[5]

Another significant function performed by the JWB in conjunction with the American Jewish Committee was the creation of the Bureau of War Records. The purpose of this organization was the collection of accurate data about Jewish participation in the war, "to serve as an instrument of morale during the conflict and as an enduring memorial after the war."[6] The process used to collect and verify the data was sophisticated. Jewish fraternal, industrial, and religious groups supplied detailed information about their Jewish members in the war. Military furlough records for Jewish holidays, as well as records from the Graves Registration Bureau, provided additional numbers to help in the collection of accurate figures.[7]

The bureau initially collected more than half a million records. These documents were further divided by name, branch of service, and hometown. The bureau concluded that between 200,000 and 225,000 Jews had served in the war. The conclusions of the bureau were remarkable. Jews, who constituted three percent of the United States population, had made up more than four percent of the armed forces, which by the end of the war had numbered 4,800,000. Thus Jews, including many new Americans, showed their support and allegiance to their country in dramatic and significant numbers.[8]

Two years after the war, a new military-centered board formed within the JWB: the Army and Navy Committee. This group represented leading rabbinic and community organizations. In its 1922 annual report, the committee commented on the lack of active-duty rabbis in the army or navy. The Army and Navy Committee contacted the War Department and requested chaplaincy positions for rabbis. The War Department did not accept the committee's recommendation for two reasons. First, the military had greatly reduced the number of available chaplaincy billets. Second, Jewish men constituted a minority of personnel at various posts and bases. The suggestion of a "roving rabbi" was rejected because "it would complicate matters from an administrative point of view and involve similar provision for other minority religious denominations."⁹ The War Department did, however, encourage rabbis to apply for commissions in the reserves. The department requested that the Army and Navy Committee screen and endorse all the rabbinic applicants. By 1922, thirteen rabbis participated as commissioned officers in the reserves.

To compensate for the lack of active-duty rabbis, the JWB, through its own staff, organized High Holiday and other observances at a number of stateside and overseas posts and bases. Some of these workers were ordained rabbis who functioned in place of military rabbis.

Although rabbis were allowed to enter the reserves, the country as a whole was becoming less hospitable. Once the war had been concluded, forces for national unity and cohesiveness deteriorated rapidly. Intolerance, nationalism, and prejudice once again dominated the thinking of many Americans. One area in which these attitudes resurfaced was immigration policy. For decades prior to the First World War, restrictionists and others had lobbied Congress for laws impeding the pace of immigration. Proponents of racial theories favoring people from Nordic countries, as opposed to individuals from eastern and southern Europe, chose the time after the war to repeat their arguments and request that the doors to America be closed to some. By 1921 and 1924, such arguments persuaded Congress to dramatically slow the rate and limit the types of people entering America. In 1924, the Johnson-Reed Act limited immigration for most Europeans to two percent of the U.S. population of each nationality as represented in the 1890 census. This act severely limited the number of Jews and Slavs who entered the country.¹⁰

In a world that had not achieved the universal peace promised by the League of Nations, many people endeavored to find a scapegoat for the ills of the country. For some, Jews became the focus of prejudicial and stereotypical ideas and actions. Anti-Jewish notions came from a number of sources. Some Jewish leaders became unfairly identified with the Bolshevik Revolution and its leaders. A fear of foreign agitators deliberately upsetting the American marketplace prevailed in the 1920s. Also, Jews became the target of a virulent anti-Semitic work written in Russia at the beginning of the century, *The Protocols of the*

Elders of Zion, which portrayed them as a cabal of international bankers whose goal was the domination of the world's economy.

Prominent Americans, such as the industrialist Henry Ford, accepted and endorsed these notions. Ford utilized his newspaper, *The Dearborn Independent*, to pursue an anti-Semitic campaign. In its pages, Jews received blame for a number of topics: mocking Christian clergy, ridiculing rural life, welcoming radicalism, and teaching murder and safe-cracking. Ford and his staff collected articles about Jews and edited them into books, which were distributed across the country. These types of activities helped create and sustain anti-Jewish sentiment across the country. His paper subsequently published sections of the *Protocols*, giving further credibility to these charges.[11]

Hate groups, such as the Ku Klux Klan, promulgated many of these prejudicial notions. The Klan achieved great influence in the 1920s. It appealed to white Protestants who felt that they were the only group capable of genuine patriotism. The Klan attacked Catholics, Jews, Blacks, and most aliens. In 1925, perhaps its strongest year, it numbered approximately five million members.[12]

Prejudice soon became institutionalized in colleges and universities as well. Beginning in 1919, Ivy League colleges began implementing quotas for the number of Jewish students admitted. Soon this became standard practice at many universities and colleges. This prejudice remained for decades and was pervasive in most schools. An article written about Harvard University in the 1930s described this phenomenon: "In the United States anti-Semitic feeling has operated within the universities themselves, in the form of a prejudice which is difficult to prove and never officially proclaimed."[13] The military academies, however, were not operating under such prejudicial philosophies, and they did not accept a quota system for Jews. In response to a letter inquiring about the ethnic background of a midshipman in May 1926, the superintendent of the United States Naval Academy stated, "The United States Naval Academy is a federal institution operated under the laws of the United States with equal rights for all."[14]

Similarly, many job opportunities and vocations became almost impossible for an applicant with a Jewish name to apply for or enter.

Jews were systematically denied access to whole sectors of the economy, including commercial banking, insurance, and the public utilities industry. Often, employers used employment agencies to screen their prospective workers to ensure that Jews were not hired. This method proved so effective that out of twenty-three commercial employment agencies surveyed in 1929, "one refused to register Jews and another said it could place no Jews. Eight were discouraging because they thought their efforts would be an exercise in futility. Seven were willing to chance an effort to place Jewish clerical workers and only six said that they could find jobs for Jewish girls."[15] Many job advertisements described their positions as "Christian Only." In 1926 the American Jewish Congress secretly surveyed prospective employers to determine why they did not hire Jews. Among the forty-five people who responded, reasons for not hiring Jews spanned the gamut, from Jews being too clannish to Jews being too assimilated.[16]

During the twenties and thirties, the activities and official documents of the military served as a counterbalance to these negative societal images. The interfaith thinking and ecumenical nature of the military were particularly laudable at a time of restrictionism, isolationism, and nativism. In April 1924 the House and Senate Subcommittees of the Committee of Military Affairs held hearings about increasing the number of active-duty chaplain positions in the army. These positions became necessary due to the increased number of small posts and camps within the armed forces. Another change under discussion concerned altering the ratio of chaplains to personnel from one chaplain per twelve hundred people to one per eight hundred.

During this testimony, a diverse group of religious organizations participated, including the Federal Council of Churches, the Roman Catholic Military Agency, other Protestant groups, and the Jewish Welfare Board. This group of religious and military representatives offered support for these measures. When the army presented testimony, it offered a broad and inclusive definition of its military clergy: "Chaplains serve as friends, counselors and guides without discrimination to all members of the command to which they are assigned, regardless of creed or sect, and strive to promote morality, religion and good order therein. There are no denominational rivalries, for each chaplain has his definite field and specific duties."[17] The vision of these various faith communities pursuing a common agenda reflected an enlightened approach to interfaith relations.

Another proposal initiated at this Congressional hearing involved elevating the rank of the chief army chaplain from colonel to brigadier general. In a statement to Congress concerning the validity of this and other proposals, the army chief of chaplains, John T. Axton made an emphatic statement about the practice of a diverse group of military ministers being supervised by a single chaplain. "Fortunately the experiences of the World War had demonstrated that Army chaplains of all creeds could work together under one ecclesiastical head who had surrounded himself with advisors representative of the various schools of religious thought . . . they can magnify points of agreement and unite to develop and strengthen those things which men hold in common as being essential to the spiritual welfare of the Army. There have been no conflicts."[18]

The Chaplain Corps's concern for interfaith sensitivity was reflected in a 1926 chaplains' training manual. The book addressed the notion of religious awareness: "The United States Government clearly expects each chaplain to be conscientious in the performance of his sacred duties and to maintain a high ideal of his obligations to all the religious needs of his military family."[19] This text recommended two Sunday morning services. The first fulfilled specific denominational requirements. The second functioned as a general religious service for the benefit of all personnel: "The Chaplain is the servant of God for all, and no narrow sectarian spirit should color his utterances, nor should his personal work assist only a special group."[20] Another section of this guide included an explanation of Jewish holidays. The responsibility rested with the Christian chaplains to ensure that, in the absence of a rabbi, Jewish personnel's spiritual needs were met.

It is clear that the attitude of the soldier or sailor would be positively enhanced upon seeing this democracy in action. In a place where esprit de corps is so significant, the troops saw their religious leaders living out this ideal of unit cooperation. The military concept of responsibility of one person for the next was magnified and personified by the attitudes and actions of most military spiritual guides and their welfare agencies. They ministered to all. It would be logical to suggest that such an attitude would have been partially responsible for any battle success the troops realized.

The manual also identified the different religious organizations that endorsed chaplains for appointment to the military. In addition to the mainline Protestant, Catholic, and Jewish agencies, these faith groups included the Unitarian Church and the Christian Scientist Church. This wide-ranging acceptance of different denominations reflected the idea that these men were the spiritual leaders for everyone. In addition to conducting divine services and offering counseling, military clergy had other tasks. These included administering educational activities, visiting with the sick and dying, and other programs associated with the general morale of the troops. Chaplains also provided entertainment for the men, utilizing motion picture projectors, record players, and slide projectors.[21]

Armed forces clergy also participated in the Civilian Conservation Corps. Initiated in 1933 as part of the New Deal, these camps provided employment and military-style training to civilians. Military chaplains led courses on citizenship and morality, which were major components of the curriculum, with rabbis participating. In 1936 there were fifteen rabbis who had been contracted by the JWB to work with the young men in such camps. Out of the three hundred thousand people in the program, over 2,200 were Jewish.[22]

In addition to the military's active influence as a counter force against the prevailing forms of racism and prejudice, other groups engaged in active opposition. The National Council of Christians and Jews, founded in 1927, had as one of its founding principles the following: "To ascertain the causes of racial ill will and to see how they could be removed or mitigated; to establish contacts between Jews and Christians where feasible and to further understandings between them."[23] A typical seminar sponsored by this group involved clergy of all faiths in discussions of common historical traditions, intergroup relations, preaching, and interfaith similarities. Despite the efforts of such groups, the Depression decade of the thirties was not noteworthy for its programs and initiatives for fighting racism or ethnic animosities.

The anti-Semitism of the thirties manifested itself in different ways.

In a 1932 analysis by the American Jewish Committee, the origin of contemporary anti-Semitism was described in somber terms: "It is a mass psychosis, more virulent than many other mass psychoses, the remedy for which will only be produced by rational attitudes of ethnic groups toward one another."[24] One source of anti-Semitism was groups associated with Nazism. Organizations such as the German-American Bund often promulgated racist, anti-Jewish pronouncements and programs. Despite its affinity for Nazi-like, storm-trooper uniforms and its relatively small number of adherents, in February 1939 this group, on the occasion of Washington's birthday, attracted over nineteen thousand people to a rally in Madison Square Garden. Disregarding a pledge by the group to be fair in their remarks, every speaker indulged in anti-Semitic threats and polemics. The Bund occasionally held joint meetings and rallies with hate groups such as the Ku Klux Klan. While the actual membership in these organizations remained small, their ideas were spread widely through the sale of tracts and other literature.[25]

In addition to these groups, individuals, some of whom were clergy, also spent much of their time advocating anti-Semitism. Perhaps the best example of this sort was Father Charles Coughlin, a Catholic priest from Detroit. In the early 1930s, Coughlin, using the new medium of radio, developed a vast following. In 1933 he required over one hundred people to handle the correspondence generated by his broadcasts. By 1938, over sixty-three radio stations across the country carried his program. In November of that year, the tenor of his radio broadcast became aggressive toward Jews. In attempting to explain the reasons for attacks against Jews and their synagogues in Germany known as *Kristallnacht*, or "The Night of the Broken Glass," Coughlin made two stereotypical charges. The first asserted that Jewish bankers in New York had financed the Russian Revolution. The second suggested that Jews manipulated the American news media and somehow controlled the way people thought.[26]

After this broadcast a number of organizations, Jewish and other, attempted to refute Father Coughlin. Some proved that much of his information came directly from German propaganda sources. Nonetheless, Father Coughlin and his broadcasts indicated the mood of the country and the depth of its anti-Semitism. The reason for Coughlin's embrace of anti-Semitic advocacy remains unclear. One scholar, Mary Athans, has suggested that Coughlin was significantly influenced by an Irish priest, Father Dennis Fahey. Fahey had published a number of anti-Jewish and pro-Nazi pamphlets. His printed ideas were very similar to those expressed by Father Coughlin.[27]

This pervasive anti-Semitism was manifested on a political level; in some cases, lives were endangered. In 1939, in the aftermath of Kristallnacht, Congress proposed a child refugee bill. This bill would have allowed ten thousand children, mostly Jewish, into the country for the duration of the war. Initially there was an immediate and impressive humanitarian response to the bill. Yet formidable opposition arose. Groups such as the Allied Patriotic Society offered testimony against the refugees. They suggested that the bill's intent was not to help all refugees, but only Jews. This assertion made the bill politically unacceptable, and it did not pass Congress.[28]

While Father Coughlin and others advanced anti-Jewish theories, other forces were quietly promoting tolerance and equality. Rabbis continued to join the military through its Reserve Chaplain Corps, and they taught interfaith understanding and mutual respect. By 1936 nineteen rabbis were participating in the reserves. Some of these rabbis held positions of great importance. Rabbi Benjamin A. Tintner, a major in the army reserves, was appointed as the first rabbi to provide biweekly services for Jewish cadets at the United States Military Academy at West Point.[29] A similar effort to have a reserve rabbi conduct services at the United States Naval Academy in Annapolis received a different response. The senior academy chaplain felt that the Jewish midshipmen's spiritual needs were met by marching into town on a Sunday morning for services at a local synagogue. This system remained in place at Annapolis until the assignment in 1987 of its first full-time, active-duty rabbi, Chaplain Norman Auerback.

The JWB maintained an ongoing commitment to the needs of Jews in the military. As war in Europe became a reality, the board drafted a number of farsighted plans that dealt with the rejuvenation of its scope and responsibilities. In the summer of 1939, leaders of the board developed a "Mobilization Plan." It involved an expansion of the Army and

Navy Committee of the JWB. JWB field-workers spread across ι. country, organizing Jewish communities in the vicinity of military camps and bases. Secretary of War Henry L. Stimson reconfirmed their status as "the official representative of the Jewish religious groups in matters pertaining to the religious and moral welfare of Jews in the Army."[30] The number of rabbis slowly increased as the war escalated.

The interwar decades were years when anti-Semitism in varying forms flourished in America. Yet the military, through its Chaplain Corps, continued to articulate the notions of mutuality and reciprocity. Throughout these years the JWB maintained a strong relationship with Jews in the armed forces and also with rabbis in the reserves. As the nation and world moved toward another world war, Jews and their rabbis were preparing to answer their country's call once again.

6

The World at War Again

By the onset of the Second World War, Jewish participation in the military had met several historical challenges. In the Civil War, the Jewish community had fought for rabbis to be legally included within the ranks of the chaplaincy. By the First World War, the Jewish community's abiding interest with their coreligionists in the armed forces had helped bring about the National Jewish Welfare Board. During the Second World War, over three hundred rabbis served in the military, ministering directly to over 550,000 Jews and millions of other service personnel.[1] These rabbis in uniform became involved in a myriad of concerns: confronting contemporary anti-Semitism, fulfilling their roles as rabbis and general spiritual mentors in war, saving the lives of thousands of Holocaust victims, and in a few instances, making the ultimate patriotic sacrifice for their country.

By 1938 Europe was faced with an ever-increasingly belligerent Germany, which first annexed Austria and then enveloped Czechoslovakia. Subsequently, the German blitzkrieg attack on Poland, followed by rapid conquests of Denmark, Norway, and France, caused the United States to galvanize its resources to prepare for a war of immense proportions. In 1940 Congress began passing larger appropriations for the military. President Roosevelt initiated industrial-military planning meetings, anticipating the cooperation of major industries in any war effort. By fall, the National Guard and other reserve units were mobilized to serve a year of active duty. A bill authorizing a one-year conscription quickly passed through Congress.[2]

America began the Second World War with a million and a half men in uniform; by the war's conclusion, over eight million people had joined the armed forces.[3] Training, equipping, and caring for these men and women represented an almost insurmountable task. A substantial amount of the spiritual care of military personnel was the responsibility of the army and navy chaplain corps.

As the army enlarged with reservists called to active duty, the chaplaincy program experienced a parallel growth. Many of the officers, including chaplains, received "temporary appointments" placing them on active duty for the duration of the war. By the attack on Pearl Harbor, almost one thousand five hundred clergy were in service, while at the war's end, this number had increased to eight thousand.[4] To ensure a wide and fair distribution of chaplaincy positions, the army devised a quota system based on the 1936 census figures.

This procedure identified the forty faith groups most prevalent in the military. In accordance with these figures, each group received a proportional amount of clergy. Roman Catholics represented the army's largest group, with over thirty percent of the allowable chaplaincy positions. Other Protestant denominations followed the Catholics. Judaism was the fifth largest group, with a quota of almost four percent. In some instances, a particular group did not fill their allotment of clergy positions and other faith communities utilized the extra numbers.[5] The navy's share of clergymen was three thousand. The Jewish percentage, 0.8 percent, was considerably lower than its percentage in the army.[6] Of the 311 rabbis who participated in the Second World War, over two-thirds served in the army.

The army's chaplains' school was at Harvard University. The curriculum included military law, map-reading, defense against chemical attacks, and physical conditioning. One part of the course included crawling through mud as bullets were fired over the clergymen's heads. Clerics serving with the Army Air Forces received additional weeks of training. To foster interfaith awareness, school officials engineered room assignments to ensure that clergy of different faith traditions roomed together.[7]

The navy established its chaplains' school at the Norfolk Naval Base; in 1943 it moved to the College of William and Mary. Chaplains were taught military thinking and terminology. Walls of a building became bulkheads, toilets became heads, and the floor, a deck.[8] The two-month course also included information about naval history, welfare agencies, the navy's disciplinary system, and survival techniques for use when abandoning ship and swimming through burning oil. Chaplains received copies of the necessary prayers for the dying, which under battle circumstances could be offered by any cleric.

From the first day of the war at Pearl Harbor, military clergy were present. During the attack, two navy chaplains died as they went down with their respective ships. Also, Chaplain H. M. Forgy, stationed on the cruiser *New Orleans*, was encouraging the ship's gunners to continue lifting hundred-pound shells for the ship's anti-aircraft batteries. His repetition of the phrases "Praise the Lord," and "Pass the Ammunition" received national publicity.[9] Throughout the war, chaplains conducted services, counseled personnel and their families, parachuted into battle, served in prisoner-of-war camps, and prayed both with and for thousands of dead and dying troops. They brought comfort, solace, and hope.

Rabbis, lay leaders, and the Jewish community were part of this chaplaincy activity. As in the First World War, the JWB initiated a concerted effort to involve most of the American-Jewish community in its war activities. The Army and Navy Committee of the JWB represented thirty-seven Jewish organizations. Over three hundred Jewish Community Centers (JCC) participated as well. This power base helped create an efficient welfare agency. The board set up facilities near major military bases and posts. By the conclusion of the war, almost every local community center had a direct connection with some aspect of the JWB.

The JWB also worked with the United Services Organization (USO), joining with other welfare agencies, such as the Young Men and Women's Christian Association, Salvation Army, and National Catholic Community Service, in fundraising and programming for the massive operation devoted to helping military personnel and their families. As the war progressed, the JWB hired individuals to work on the USO staff as well.[10]

The JWB developed a number of subcommittees that focused the war efforts of the wider community. These groups included the Committee on Religious Activities, the Publications Committee, the

Women's Division, the Bureau of War Records, the Army and Navy Public Relations Committee, the Committee on Personal Service, and a Veterans Service Committee.[11] As it had in the First World War, the JWB drafted plans to build recreational facilities and to train field-workers to assist the work of the Jewish chaplains.

The Committee on Religious Activities (CRA) had a direct impact on the lives of service personnel. In 1940 David de Sola Pool, an Orthodox rabbi of the Sephardic tradition, led this major group. He brought many qualifications to this role. In the First World War, he had served as a field organizer and director of army camp work for the JWB. In the interwar years, he held significant leadership positions with the New York Board of Rabbis and the Synagogue Council of America; he was also the president of the Union of Sephardic Congregations of America. Rabbi de Sola Pool's stature in the Jewish and secular communities constituted a crucial element in the substantial accomplishments of his committee.

The CRA's mission was to address the single issue of how best to meet the religious needs of Jewish service personnel. The CRA's tasks included the recruitment and endorsement of rabbis for service as military chaplains, the supplying of prayer books and other liturgical items, and the coordination of the armed forces' policies for religious observances and holiday furloughs. The CRA determined that, as much as possible, its policies and decisions should represent equally the three major branches in Judaism: Orthodox, Conservative, and Reform. This decision had many ramifications. As the war progressed, a host of concerns related to Judaism arose. In almost all of the cases, the JWB responded with a united voice, which reflected a spirit of intra-Jewish cooperation that was highly unusual. However, not everyone in the Jewish community accepted the leadership role of the CRA.

In March 1941 a small group of Orthodox rabbis, the Federation of Orthodox Rabbis in America, complained to the War Department about chaplaincy requirements. Becoming a military cleric required a bachelor's degree and three years of theological training. However, according to Orthodox tradition, a man received rabbinical ordination through proving proficiency in certain Talmudic (Rabbinic) texts. Obtaining a secular college degree was irrelevant to this process. This lack of a degree, they maintained, disqualified such individuals from chaplaincy service.

This association disapproved of the JWB, primarily because of its inclusion of Conservative and Reform rabbis, which this group considered as not authentically rabbinic. As Rabbi Lev noted, "Reform and Conservative are by no means regarded by the Orthodox rabbinical boards and people as well as rabbis in the true sense of Rabbinical leadership, or rabbis in Israel, neither in private affairs, and especially not in army life."[12] The federation requested a meeting with Rabbi Lev and the army's chief of chaplains. The response from the chief of chaplains as reported by Lev was clear. The Jewish Welfare Board was the sole recognized civilian agency that dealt with the Jewish chaplaincy and related issues. While rabbis from this federation received permission to speak in military bases throughout the New York area, no further correspondence with the JWB was undertaken.

Regarding the issue of Orthodox rabbis serving as military chaplains, Rabbi Samuel Berilant, president of the Orthodox Rabbinical Council of America and a member of the JWB, asked Dr. Joseph B. Soloveitchik to offer counsel. Rabbi Soloveitchik was recognized as a master of rabbinic law. His responses to such questions affected people's religious practices and life decisions. His answer was emphatic: "It is not only permissible, but it is also the duty of every Orthodox rabbi to enlist in the armed forces for the purpose of rendering spiritual guidance to Jewish soldiers."[13] Thus, while some dissatisfaction with the JWB existed, the vast majority of Jews in America appeared to feel that it represented their needs.

The JWB also recommended to the army that a rabbi be assigned to its chief of chaplains' staff to serve as a liaison between the two organizations. This proposal was accepted, and Chaplain Aryeh Lev served in that position for most of the war. Lev's position proved significant, as he had a direct role in the training, assignments, and careers of hundreds of Jewish chaplains. The navy did not have a rabbi on its chief of chaplain's staff, although Chaplain Joshua Goldberg, the senior-ranking rabbi, served unofficially in that role.[14]

During World War II, anti-Semitic rumors continued to be an issue confronting the Jewish community. Some stories suggested that Jews were not fulfilling their patriotic obligations. Others averred that Jewish doctors granted medical exemptions for Jews. The JWB created the Army and Navy Public Relations Committee to address this phenomenon. It set three major goals: first, to inform the general public that Jews fully participated in the national defense; second, to verify and counter anti-Semitic rumors related to military issues; third, to educate the Jewish community about the spiritual and welfare needs of Jews in service. This committee used the media whenever possible to spread its messages. News items about interfaith cooperation, such as one about Jewish soldiers taking duty on Christmas Day, were one of the types of stories used to rebut anti-Semitic charges. This committee included representatives from the American Jewish Committee, the Anti-Defamation League of B'nai Brith, the Jewish War Veterans, and other Jewish fraternal groups, and these representatives worked together on local and national levels.[15]

As mentioned above, the recruiting of rabbis for service was a high priority for the Committee for Religious Activities. In the summer of 1941, Rabbi Lev, representing the JWB and the army's chief of chaplains' office, went to rabbinic conferences to promote the chaplaincy. His presentations were informational and inspirational: "Once again, our national need has dissolved the barriers between man and man. They gather under freedom's banner forgetting their differences, remembering their common liberties. They stand shoulder to shoulder, bound in a new comradeship."[16] The rabbis raised a number of issues in conjunction with their potential military service. Job security was a primary concern. The rabbis wanted to ensure that those individuals who volunteered for service would have jobs upon their return. Because of such concerns and despite Lev's campaigns and the changing situation in Europe, rabbis were slow to enter the chaplaincy.

To compensate partially for the lack of active-duty rabbis, the JWB announced that some civilian rabbis would take positions at military posts for the summer months. These rabbis served under the aegis of the JWB and had no military rank, but met the religious needs of soldiers and sailors. An August 1941 letter from James G. Heller, a veteran chaplain in World War One and president of the Central

Conference of American Rabbis (the Reform rabbinic organization), reflected his concern about the lack of rabbinic commitment to the armed forces:

> We rabbis are falling down in an important national responsibility. Our boys are deprived of vital help and there is a great danger of creating a harmful and unjust attitude to our people in the Army and in the nation as a whole. . . . Thousands of our boys are asking why there are no rabbis in their camps to conduct services and provide counsel and guidance in the same way that the Christian boys are receiving. . . . This is a call in the name of our faith, our country and our people.[17]

Heller's letter went on to detail the pay and role of chaplains. It also addressed concerns about job security upon return from service. But the problem of recruiting rabbis into the service became a moot point after Pearl Harbor. Within days of the attack, rabbis volunteered in record numbers for service, as did millions of others.

Other faith groups underwent similar experiences in trying to secure acceptable numbers of chaplains. In April 1941 the military vicar, Archbishop Francis J. Spellman, became involved in recruiting priests for the military. A special appeal for priests was sent throughout the country: "The need for priests is still great. Posts with 2,000 Catholics have been left for weeks without Catholic chaplains . . . not a single transport has a Catholic chaplain because there are none to spare."[18] When the war began, over five hundred priests served on active duty; this number grew to 3,200 by the war's conclusion.

In January 1942 the Committee of Religious Activities was reorganized and renamed the Committee on Army and Navy Activities (CANRA). A new executive director, Rabbi Philip Bernstein, took on the daily administration of this expanding program. Within months the CANRA became involved in several projects: the republication of a Jewish armed forces prayer book and Bible, the provision of Kosher food supplies for the troops, the writing of religious messages for Jewish and Christian chaplains, and the arranging of on-site visits with armed forces chaplains at military bases.[19]

As part of the CANRA, each rabbinic organization provided rabbis for military service. These groups used various approaches toward recruiting. The Reform movement, represented by the Central Conference of American Rabbis, used a sophisticated system for securing candidates. The movement held regular meetings with its synagogue and seminary representatives. All recent graduates received an evaluation regarding their availability for service. The order of eligibility began with single rabbis, followed by married rabbis without children, and concluding with married rabbis with children. Senior rabbis visited the graduates and informed them about their obligations regarding the chaplaincy. Congregations had agreed that, whenever a rabbi returned from service, he would take over in his prior position as soon as possible. The congregations were also asked to pay the difference between the rabbis' civilian earnings and their military pay. The Reform seminary, Hebrew Union College, also agreed to ordain its upcoming classes on an accelerated basis, providing more rabbis for the armed forces.[20]

The Conservative movement chose a voluntary draft system. It formed a rabbinic availability committee that summoned rabbis to serve in the military as the group deemed necessary. The Orthodox movement was not represented by a single seminary or rabbinical group, but its rabbis also came forth to serve. During the war, 311 rabbis served on active duty. Of this total, 147 came from the Reform movement, 96 from the Conservative, and 68 from the Orthodox.[21]

Within two months of U.S. entry into the war, the first wartime conference of military rabbis convened in Atlanta, Georgia. Eighteen rabbis (seventeen army and one navy) came together to discuss a variety of topics, including getting maximum attendance at religious services, handling military protocol, developing educational programs, and managing relationships with Christian chaplains, local Jewish organizations, and JWB welfare workers.[22] This group recommended that the JWB set aside funds to lend to Jewish men for buying Kosher food or addressing personal emergencies. The conference was a success. For the most part, the rabbis functioned in isolated duty assignments, and such meetings allowed them to pray as a rabbinic community, to share stories and ideas, and to build morale.

One of the ongoing issues affecting the Jewish chaplains was anti-Semitism. In the First World War, there had been few, if any, documented cases of anti-Jewish incidents between soldiers. But in the Second World War, many people entered the military with anti-Semitic beliefs and prejudices that had to be dispelled. One persistent prejudice was the stereotype of Jewish nonpatriotism. David Wyman has suggested that the most recurrent slander against Jews was that they avoided military service while Christian men went to war. He cites a popular ditty: "So it's onward into battle, let us send the Christian slobs. When the war is done and victory won, all the Jews will have their jobs."[23]

Nazi propagandists also promoted the theme of Jews not doing their fair share of fighting. Pamphlets dropped from airplanes to American armed forces showed a caricature of a Jewish man with his arm around a slim woman. The title of the caption, "The Girl You Left Behind," and the paragraph under the picture left no doubt as to its purpose: "Like many other home warriors he [Levy] made the grade piling up dough and growing fat on the sacrifices of young American boys fighting on foreign battlefields. . . . Bob [the soldier] was shipped to Europe to fight for the causes of Sam Levy and his kind."[24]

The National Conference of Christians and Jews worked with the armed forces to counter such allegations. In June 1942 the conference created a speakers' bureau of distinguished religious leaders from a variety of faith groups to visit military installations. In conjunction with the chaplain or the morale officer, these clerics offered their visions of America: "As children of God, we should all share a brotherhood which calls for individual and social responsibility and reciprocity. America is a demonstration of this brotherhood. Its citizens thrive in understanding, not prejudice; in mutuality, not selfishness; in giving to and receiving from each other equality of opportunity and respect for personality."[25] The conference estimated that over two million service personnel received these lectures in one year. While the ultimate success of this program was difficult to gauge, it offered the type of message needed to help address prejudicial beliefs among the troops.

In the midst of this work, the build-up of rabbis entering the armed forces continued. At the end of 1942, over one hundred rabbis were endorsed for service. Thirty-two failed to receive certification for various reasons, such as age or physical disabilities.[26] Of the hundred ac-

Jewish women in uniform played a significant role in the war effort. They are shown participating in a July 1944 service held in London by Chaplain Judah Nadich. Courtesy U.S. Army Chaplain Museum.

tive-duty rabbis, over half went to overseas assignments with combat units. This decision placed them in dangerous situations, some of which led to death.

Rabbi Alexander Goode gave his life for his country. Chaplain Goode was married and had one daughter. He was ordained in 1937, earned his Ph.D. from Johns Hopkins University in 1940, and served in civilian congregations. He entered the army in August 1942 at the age of thirty-one. After his basic training, he received orders to travel overseas to a base in Greenland. Initially, he attempted to get these orders modified, writing to Rabbi Lev in the Army Chief of Chaplains Office to suggest that other bases needed rabbis more than Greenland did. Lev responded that orders were orders, and that if the army and the JWB had determined that a need existed, then he should obey the

A commemorative stamp issued by the post office recalling the four chaplains *(left to right):* Fox, Poling, Washington, and Goode. Courtesy Marcus Center, American Jewish Archives.

orders. In a separate note to the leadership of the CANRA, Lev wrote, "This man is bitter. He is away from his family. His wife is not settled and his child may be sick . . . his mind is not at peace."[27]

Despite these concerns, Goode prepared for his departure to Greenland. In late January 1943, he, along with three other army chaplains, boarded the United States Transport Ship Dorchester with nine hundred men ordered to the European theater. At 1:00 AM on February 3, ninety miles from Greenland, a German submarine torpedoed the ship, which immediately began to sink. The soldiers, asleep below decks, were jarred awake. Within a few moments, the order came to abandon ship. The few available life boats were launched, but the abruptness of the attack, the darkness, and the chaos and panic below decks caused many of the men to come to the top decks of the ship without life jackets or gloves. Without these items they would not survive long in the frigid ocean waters. The chaplains, whose sleeping area was near the top decks of the ship, began giving their own life jackets and gloves to the panicked soldiers while offering words of encouragement in the face of catastrophe. Within minutes, according to legend, the chaplains stood arm in arm, offering final prayers as the ship sank into the dark, cold waters. In addition to Rabbi Goode, Protestant chaplains George Fox and Clark Poling and Catholic priest John Washington perished with the ship.[28]

Their bravery led to this apocryphal saying, attributed to one of the chaplains: "Take this, my son, you need it more than I do." This story of sacrifice helped lift the morale of the entire country in the winter of 1943. The chaplains were posthumously awarded the Distinguished Service Crosses for bravery.[29] Five other rabbis—Henry Goody, Samuel D. Hurwitz, Herman L. Rosen, Irving Tepper, and Louis Werfel—died defending their country during the war.[30]

This type of sacrifice, which put the welfare of the troops first, was evidenced throughout the war in countless circumstances. Rabbi Robert I. Kahn described a situation in which, as the only available chaplain, he held a prayer service for troops going into a combat area. Assembling the men, he arranged for Catholic and Protestant lay leaders to lead the appropriate prayers. He then held a brief Jewish service. Afterwards, he passed out Bibles, rosaries, and mezuzots. The soldiers took all of these items with them into combat.[31]

Chaplain Abraham Avrech, emphasizing the vast distances over which his congregation was spread, told of a Protestant chaplain who personally notified Jewish personnel about the approaching High Holidays. This chaplain also ensured that all troops desiring to attend services received furloughs. Most impressively, when he discovered that there was no Torah (Jewish sacred scroll) available for the service, the chaplain requisitioned a military plane, flew hundreds of miles, borrowed a Torah, and returned to the base in time for the commencement of services.[32]

This interfaith sensitivity extended to military chapels as well. When Congress in 1942 appropriated monies for new chapels, the army determined that they should be constructed so that all faith groups could pray comfortably within them. No permanent religious items were to be placed inside the chapels. Any paintings or religious fixtures needed to be movable, so that within a brief period, another group could utilize the chapel. This use of one house of prayer for all faiths explicitly reaffirmed mutual respect and understanding.[33]

Such issues were among those discussed when forty-two rabbis assigned with the navy and marines (navy chaplains were assigned to marine units) met in March 1943 in Norfolk, Virginia, with representatives of the CANRA for their first wartime conference. When the navy rabbis discussed anti-Semitism, the rabbis generally considered this phenomenon to represent no major difficulty for them. One of the attendees, Rabbi Joshua Goldberg, suggested that, while individuals in the military might have been anti-Semitic, the navy system was fair and reacted appropriately when an issue was raised. He further stated that the navy treated him with great dignity.[34] A JWB representative reminded the naval chaplains that all cases of suspected anti-Semitism should be forwarded to the JWB for investigation.

Another discussion centered around the requirements for a navy rabbi. The rabbis at the conference felt that Orthodox rabbis did not do well in a naval command: "The consensus seemed to be that while no general rule could be laid down, the nature of the work and the measure of the liberal adjustment required, led to the conclusion that the chaplain should come from the Reform group; the Sabbath and Kashruth [dietary laws] cannot be observed as they can in certain Army set-ups."[35]

The gathered rabbis also offered their perspectives about being a general spiritual mentor and a rabbi. Most felt that they functioned as nonsectarian ministers for most of the week. They visited hospitals, provided counseling, and maintained the morale of their entire units. Rabbi Samuel Sandmel articulated the feelings of many when he wrote, "A Naval chaplain is a chaplain to men of all faiths, and Jewish only during periods of divine services or when the problem of the consulter was specifically Jewish."[36]

A second conference of army rabbis, held in July 1943 in San Francisco, presented a forum for rabbis to express needs and concerns. One of the major topics was future assignments. Speaking for the army and the JWB, Rabbi Lev estimated that, by the end of 1943, there would be approximately 225 rabbis in the army, with over half assigned to overseas posts. This need for rabbis came from military commanders, who indicated that large numbers of Jewish wounded, as well as those killed in action, required hospitals visits or funeral duties. As stateside, active-duty rabbis received orders for overseas duty, JWB welfare workers and local community rabbis attempted to compensate for this loss of religious coverage in this country. The War Department received requests for rabbis from all parts of the globe; throughout the war, the need for rabbis overseas exceeded the supply of available rabbis.

The rabbis assembled at their second conference also spoke about the unique aspects of their ministries. In addition to the regular schedule of services, counseling, and visitations, some chaplains offered special programs. Chaplain Jacob L. Halevi wrote a special memorial service with Hebrew readings, entitled "They Shall Not Die." This liturgy, read jointly by Jewish soldiers and Christian chaplains, commemorated Jewish teenagers who had been killed in the war.[37] Other rabbis indicated their creative approaches to making contact with their men. Chaplain Robert S. Marcus met troop trains as they arrived at his unit and gave all the soldiers schedules of chaplaincy-related programs. Chaplain Martin M. Weitz took pictures of all who attended his services and made them available to be sent home to family and friends. Chaplain Isidore Barnett described his "Jeep" ministry. His troops were bivouacked in widely scattered desert areas, so he traveled from camp to camp, conducting multiple Sabbath and, as appropriate, holiday services.[38]

Rabbi Earl S. Stone exemplified a chaplain's flexibility. Assigned to an army division in Tunisia, Stone made plans for the upcoming Passover seder. The day before the holiday, he was sworn to secrecy and told that, on the night of Passover, the entire division would be on an all-night march and would make a surprise attack on a German stronghold. It would therefore be impossible to hold the seder meal. That same evening, Stone assembled his Jewish troops in the desert and offered a fascinating service:

> In an open field that night, I stood before some 300 hardened veterans of six arduous months of battle . . . I asked them to sit on the ground and to conjure up in their minds the memory of a Seder at home . . . I recited the Kiddush [prayer over wine] with an imaginary cup of wine in my hand and had everyone break an imaginary matzo [unleavened

Chaplain Robert S. Marcus, using a jeep as a *bimah* (altar), conducting services in Normandy, France, August 1944. Courtesy Jewish Welfare Board Archives.

bread]. . . . At the end of the service man after man, with tears flowing down his cheeks, bade me Gut Yontif [Happy Holiday].[39]

This type of creativity in the midst of war characterized many of the rabbis in their ministries.

In 1943 the army issued its annual chaplaincy report indicating the level of danger faced in war. Twenty-four military chaplains died in battle, while thirty-nine perished in nonbattle accidents or from illnesses; another thirty-three became prisoners of war.[40] Military clerics received 129 awards for heroism and bravery; rabbis accumulated their fair share in these categories. Dangerous conditions became a standard element in some people's ministries. Rabbi Edgar E. Siskin, serving with the Marines on Pelilu Island, described one Yom Kippur service that held plenty of risk: "The altar rigged by Chaplain Murphy, Division Chaplain, was improvised out of ammunition boxes, and was covered by a length of captured Japanese silk. . . . There we were not 200 yards from a ridge still held by the Japs, within range of sniper and mortar fire. Throughout the service the artillery kept up a shattering fire overhead."[41]

While warfare continued, the fight against societal anti-Semitism continued as well. In April 1943 a public outcry ensued over anti-Semitic references in an army-approved book of Biblical readings. The book, entitled *My Daily Readings from the New Testament*, contained a footnote that referred to Jews: "The Jews are the synagogue of Satan. The True Synagogue is the Christian Church."[42] The Protestant Textbook Commission initially brought this issue to the public's attention. The mission of this group included eliminating anti-Semitic references from textbooks. In this case, the JWB, the Military Ordinariate, and the army's chief of chaplains became involved. Within weeks the book's publishers offered an apology. While some copies had been distributed, the remaining copies were modified by removal of the offensive references.[43]

The personal correspondence of Rabbi Frank Bennett indicated the pervasive nature of anti-Semitism during the war. Bennett, in August 1943, described some of the Christian clergy he met as he entered the chaplaincy program. He wrote that most of these individuals came from small towns across America. They brought with them widely accepted stereotypes about Jews. One common belief held that Jews were wealthier than most Americans and that, if they served in the military, they did so as supply officers. When Rabbi Bennett spoke to his chaplain colleagues about the plight of Jews in Europe, he received some startling responses: "They feel sorry for the Jew but will do nothing about it. They sincerely believe Jewish suffering is part of God's will and who are they to oppose the will of God. Jewish suffering is due to either (a) punishment for rejecting Jesus or (b) as a necessary principle for the second coming."[44]

Part of Chaplain Bennett's job, as well as that of most military rabbis, involved confronting and changing such beliefs by educating

Battle-weary troops gathered on Pelilu Island for prayers led by Chaplain Edgar E. Siskin. Courtesy Jewish Welfare Board Archives.

fellow clergy about Judaism and its tenets. Navy chaplain Joshua Goldberg noted that he went to the navy's chaplains' school at William and Mary College on a regular basis throughout the war. During these visits, he and a Catholic chaplain engaged in a friendly debate about various tenets of their religions. Goldberg said that the Protestant clergy, especially the Baptists, "loved it."[45]

Working with other clergy and addressing issues such as anti-Semitism added pressure to an already difficult environment. The stressful toll of war, in addition to separation from family and friends, led some chaplains to experience physical and emotional breakdowns. In a few instances, clergy who were in overseas assignments returned to the states as medical patients. A very small number of rabbis suffered in this manner. Another factor and one that particularly affected rabbis were the large geographical areas they covered in order to minister to

Chaplain Elliot Davis standing on a crate while leading Yom Kippur (Day of Atonement) services on New Georgia Island in the South Pacific, October 9, 1943. Courtesy U.S. Army Chaplain Museum.

a widely scattered congregation. In one case, as a result of a series of unusual personal and military circumstances, a rabbi had been separated from his family for four years. Medical discharges or humanitarian transfers to stateside bases were utilized to solve such difficult problems. For the most part, however, military rabbis performed their duties and made the most of their circumstances.

The career of Rabbi Harold E. Gordon illustrates one unique military ministry. In 1944 a senior chaplain asked Chaplain Gordon if he liked air travel. Having flown once and enjoyed it, Rabbi Gordon answered in the affirmative. Within a few months, he received orders to the Army Air Force and a chaplaincy assignment that covered an immense geographical area. One typical ministry circuit took him from a home base in Maine to Canada; Labrador; Newfoundland; Greenland; Iceland; Prestwick (Scotland); the Azores; Bermuda; New York City; and Manchester, New Hampshire.[46] Throughout these travels, Rabbi Gordon carried, in addition to his personal gear, religious supplies, Jewish periodicals, Kosher snacks, and a portable Torah. He used this Torah as the spiritual anchor for the religious services he conducted. Kept in a separate travel box, this Torah became known as "The Flying Torah." While most rabbis did not travel as widely as Rabbi Gordon, they did cover wide areas to reach their far-flung congregants.

As these military rabbis traveled around the world, one of their most essential areas of responsibility concerned questions of Jewish law and rituals. Under war-related circumstances, certain Jewish observances proved difficult to maintain. Throughout the war, questions of Jewish practice arose from several sources: the chiefs of chaplains offices, civilian and military rabbis, and of course the troops themselves. In Jewish tradition, this process of asking and answering questions is known as "responsa." In responsa literature, questions asked and then answered by prominent rabbinical leaders often had the force of religious law and became the normative practice for Jews.

The Responsa Committee formed by the JWB faced difficult tasks. First, it operated, as noted previously, on a tri-rabbinic level, attempting to represent all three movements in Judaism. This was a daunting task, as each Jewish movement viewed Jewish traditions and religious requirements from differing perspectives. Yet these different viewpoints were all reflected in the answers offered by the responsa committee. A second challenge concerned the questions themselves. When the committee members responded to a question, they qualified their answer by informing the civilian community that their answers referred to a war's emergency circumstances and were not applicable to a peacetime

Chaplain Harold H. Gordon *(far right)* arrives at a base in the far northern area of the North Atlantic as part of his ministry in the Air Transport Command. Courtesy Jewish Welfare Board Archives.

setting. For example, questions about maintaining the laws of kashrut (Jewish dietary laws) or the rules for the Sabbath day might be more likely to be relaxed due to the war, while in a civilian setting the allowances for altering such laws were much more limited. The committee, over the course of the war, responded to a number of topics, including questions about the permissibility of performing a marriage on a Friday night, or over the phone; conversions; Friday evening services in the Arctic regions; conscientious objectors; and funeral and burial practices.[47]

The Responsa Committee, comprised of Rabbis Solomon B. Free-

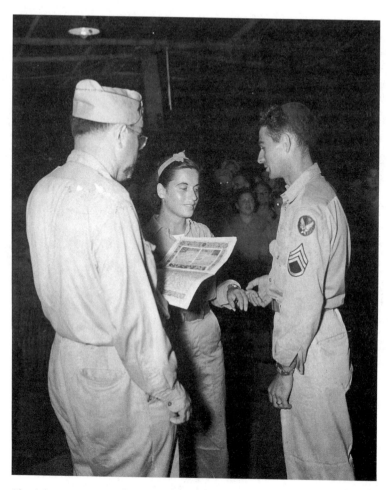

Chaplain Morris Adler reading a *ketubah* (marriage contract) at a wedding in the Western Pacific. Staff Sergeant Harry Becker marries Corporal Evelyn M. Cowan, March 1945. Courtesy Jewish Welfare Board Archives.

hof, Leo Jung, and Milton Steinberg, followed a set pattern when a question was asked. Jewish traditions were studied to ascertain if the question had been addressed historically and in what context. Any precedents from the tradition were then reconciled with the wartime experiences presented to the rabbis on the committee. In this manner they responded to most of the questions directed to them. The following is a typical question to which the committee responded.

A military rabbi wrote asking if burial on the Sabbath was ever permissible and if it was allowed during wartime. This question was raised after the crash of a military plane in which a number of men were killed, including a Jewish soldier. The bodies, mangled and inseparable, were to be buried in a mass grave. The authorities made all the arrangements for a joint memorial service and funeral to take place as soon as possible. The service was arranged for a Saturday (the Jewish Sabbath). The rabbi had told the organizers that he could participate in the military aspects of the service but not offer any prayers, because Jewish tradition expressly forbade burial on the Sabbath.[48]

The committee's response was measured and sensitive. First it reviewed Talmudic tradition and reinforced the idea that burials, even if they are performed by non-Jews, are not accepted on the Sabbath. "Logically it ought to be permitted to bury the dead on the Sabbath, but since it is ugly and shameful to be buried on the Sabbath, in violation of Jewish law, it is forbidden also for burial to be performed by Gentiles."[49] After establishing this principle, the committee then referred to another rabbinic authority, the Chofetz Chayyim, who wrote that, if the government orders the immediate burial of someone due to an epidemic, then the burial must take place, even on the Sabbath. Therefore, "With regard to a man in military life, the duties imposed by the command of the government, *tsivvui hammemshalah*, are permitted to be done and he is thereby not a profaner of the Sabbath."[50]

The committee concluded that, in a battlefield situation, the Jewish chaplain and any other Jewish soldiers who were so ordered must bury the dead, even on the Sabbath. The committee somewhat qualified their conclusion by recommending that, if possible, the rabbi ask for a

Grave markers for Jewish and Christian armed-forces personnel at a military cemetery on the island of Oahu, Hawaii, end of World War Two. Courtesy Jewish Welfare Board Archives.

one-day delay of the service, or, if the service did take place on a Saturday, that sections of the liturgy be modified to reflect the fact that they were offered on the Sabbath. This type of sage advice prevailed throughout the war.

Catholic religious authorities underwent a similar process. Archbishop Spellman, head of the Military Ordinariate, received ecclesiastical permission for a number of liturgical changes for Catholic personnel. Military chapels used by other faiths became acceptable for Catholic services. Changes were allowed concerning the time of Mass. Because of troop movement at night and the rapidity of battle, permission for Mass to be held at any time of the day or night became acceptable. As with the JWB, concern existed that this exception be understood as a temporary one: "The privilege, however, had to be used only for the benefit of military personnel in the strict sense . . . it did not apply to civilians of any group, no matter how closely they were related to the military establishment."[51] The JWB, the Military Ordinariate, and other faith traditions attempted constantly to reconcile their religious requirements with the everchanging realities of war.

One of the most significant religious areas dealt with during the war was that of proper burials and grave markings for all personnel. In the middle of the war, the CANRA notified the War Department that it had selectively studied death records. This committee concluded that nearly half of the Jewish soldiers killed in battle had been buried without the benefit of a Jewish funeral ceremony or an appropriate grave marker. Different factors contributed to this phenomenon. First, some Jewish soldiers removed their dog tags, which designated them as Jewish, for fear of what might happen if they were captured by the Germans. Others died in explosions, in crashes, or at sea, which made proper identification impossible. Paperwork that verified religious preference was often unavailable at the time of a burial service. Finally, a rabbi may not have been present to officiate.[52] To remedy this situation, Chief of Staff General George Marshall directed that Jewish chaplains in each theater of war be afforded the opportunity to visit cemeteries in their commands. The rabbis placed Jewish grave markers where appropriate and offered memorial services. After the completion of these rituals, the army changed the official military records to reflect the Jewish services.

As mentioned earlier, anti-Semitism persisted throughout the war in a variety of places and situations. By 1944, the JWB's Bureau of War Records had devised an elaborate system of local committees that reported almost every instance of Jews receiving military honors, such as the declaring of war heroes, or of war-related deaths or injuries among Jews. These committees also reported Jewish military personnel who had become prisoners of war. The committee kept these numbers to refute all sorts of anti-Semitic notions. It also collected information on the ratio of Jewish to non-Jewish dentists in the military, the percentage of Jews in the navy and marines, and the number of Jews who received deferments for agricultural service. Near the end of the war, this group utilized early International Business Machines (IBM) technology to quantify their data.[53]

As the final year of the war began, the need for more rabbis was reflected in official messages. General Dwight Eisenhower requested fifty additional rabbis for the European theater. Military and civilian hospitals needed rabbis to work with recuperating Jewish soldiers and with troops heading into battle. The chief of chaplains responded that the army could not meet the number requested; however, they would send as many as possible. At the same time, commanders in the Pacific theater also requested more rabbis. The JWB recommended to the military that rabbis in stateside bases be ordered overseas. It also coordinated a new attempt to recruit rabbis for the military and solicited civilian rabbis to support military bases stateside in place of rabbis going overseas.

In light of a persistent need for more rabbis and their difficult job requirements, the continual support of Christian colleagues, as previously noted, proved essential. Performing joint funeral ceremonies, sharing counseling cases, and working as members of the military chaplains' team represented the norm for most chaplains. Herschel Schacter, an Orthodox rabbi, served three years in the army. During these years he recalled that his fellow chaplains assisted him on numerous occasions. He did not recall any personal or professional instances of anti-Semitism.[54]

However, in some isolated cases, problems existed. In April 1945 Father Thomas Bryant, a Catholic chaplain, was asked to provide volunteers to assist in the preparation of the Passover seder. Chaplain Bryant did not comply with this request and received a letter of reprimand from his commanding officer. In a letter to the army chief of chaplains, Father Bryant explained his actions: "Since the Colonel did not agree with our attitude and considered it uncharitable and being exclusive on our part, I had to explain that since we Catholics considered our religion true, we could not take part in religious services of a religion we considered false."[55]

Perhaps the most memorable incident of this kind occurred in the Pacific Theater with Rabbi Roland B. Gittelsohn, a navy chaplain serving with the marines on Iwo Jima. Throughout the spring, the marines had been involved in major battles in the Pacific. In May 1945 Chaplain Gittelsohn's senior chaplain asked him to deliver the main

First Jewish services held in Germany in the middle of concrete Dragon-teeth tank barriers. Chaplain Sidney Lefkowitz, October 1944. Courtesy U.S. Army Chaplain Museum.

address at the dedication of the Fifth Marine Division cemetery at Iwo Jima. When this news reached the other navy chaplains, a majority objected. They believed that a Jewish chaplain should not offer prayers over Christian marines. They stated that they would advise their congregants not to attend if the rabbi spoke.

After he heard of this dissension, Rabbi Gittelsohn requested that the senior chaplain get a replacement speaker. He delivered the address that he had prepared for the main dedication to a small group of

Chaplain Morris A. Frank conducts service for secular New Year with troops advancing into Germany, January 1, 1945. Courtesy U.S. Army Chaplain Museum.

Jewish soldiers and a few Protestant chaplains who had sided with him. One of these chaplains borrowed a copy of his speech, reproduced it, and distributed it among the marines. Some of these copies were sent stateside, where the speech received prominent press coverage and further dissemination. Chaplain Gittelsohn's words, stated so eloquently, are still powerful: "Indeed here lie officers and men, Negroes and whites, rich and poor together. Here are Protestants, Catholics and Jews, together. Here no man prefers another because of his faith, or despises him because of his color.... Among these men there is no discrimination, no prejudice, no hatred. Theirs is the highest and purest democracy."[56] In a later description of this incident, Rabbi Gittelsohn recounted that, although there was much animosity directed toward him, it was not necessarily because he was a Jew. He suggested that many of the chaplains were hostile to him because of his affinity with black soldiers and his liberal views in general.[57]

These instances of noncooperation were the exception rather than the rule among chaplains. In fact, the large majority of Jewish chaplains spoke of the remarkable cooperation they received from their Christian co-workers. As noted by Rabbi Morris N. Kertzer, "Somewhere in the history of the Jewish military chaplaincy there should be recorded the simple fact that our ministration to the half-million or more men entrusted to us would never have been possible were it not for the active help and blessing of our Christian colleagues."[58]

In the final campaigns of the war, military rabbis played a lifesaving role for thousands of people. As Allied armies swept across Europe toward a meeting with Russian forces and the final defeat of Nazism, they liberated country after country. In many areas they found concentration camps with gas chambers, and crematoria still filled with victims. Many of these individuals were more dead than alive. These Holocaust survivors, along with other victims of the concentration camps, were designated "displaced persons."[59] The Allies presumed that, once liberated, these victims would want to return to their countries of origin. This did not apply to many Jews. They had suffered harsh discrimination in their indigenous countries and had no desire to return.

In many instances, military rabbis accompanied the advancing armies. They quickly began functioning as unofficial points of contact between the military authorities and the victims. The needs of the survivors were enormous: adequate food and shelter, medical supplies, the reestablishing of religious and social services, help attempting to find out if loved ones had survived, the reuniting of families, and the caring for orphans created by the Holocaust. Many agencies with the responsibility of aiding the victims, such as the (American Jewish) Joint Distribution Committee, had much difficulty getting organized across Europe to meet these needs.

Military rabbis attempted to meet some of these pressing human needs. Rabbi Lee Levinger, a veteran of the First World War, gave an account of some of the difficulties the rabbis faced: "The needs were

endless—legal status, housing, clothing, food. . . . For months no civilian organization was permitted in the occupied areas, while the army
was not organized to care for vast numbers of Displaced Persons, but
to win wars."[60] In the days and weeks after liberation and before international agencies began to effectively operate, individual Jewish chaplains, with the help of fellow clerics, and individual soldiers made a
vast difference in saving the lives of these victims. Each rabbi, depending upon his location and circumstances, did something for the welfare
and strengthening of these survivors. Often, the rabbis had to bend
some of the military rules that they normally followed. This bending
of rules, sometimes with the knowledge of their superior officers, saved
lives and put their careers at risk.

Chaplain Ernst Lorge was assigned to the Sixty-ninth Division. In
May and June 1945, he assisted over one thousand women who had
survived Auschwitz. With the assistance of his general, he ensured that
the women were moved into displaced persons camps and assisted with
food supplies. When the women discovered that the Americans were
leaving the region and that the Russians would be taking over, they
besieged Rabbi Lorge with requests that they not be left behind. The
army provided special trains to move the women who wished to go to
the American zone. However, there was a group of Jews who were
hospitalized. They vowed to commit suicide unless they were allowed
to leave as well. While army rules did not allow for patients to be
moved without proper authorization, Chaplain Lorge, with the help of
Jewish soldiers, found trucks and moved the patients to a safe location.[61]

Others, such as Rabbi Herbert Eskin, resorted to different means to
save lives. Eskin was assigned with the 100th Infantry Division in Stuttgart, Germany. With the assistance of the mayor of Stuttgart, he established a committee to organize relief work to help refugees and survivors. He also established a relief home and refugee center. Room,
board, and clothing were provided to those in need. In the first weeks
after liberation, Eskin was given food for the center from local farmers
and grocers. However, after these supplies were used, it became very
difficult to obtain further food. He used other means to gather the
needed supplies. At night, he and a small group of Jewish soldiers

would go to different villages and force farmers at gunpoint to slaughter cattle and prepare them for cooking. On the way back, they raided a grocery store and took necessary supplies. The transportation used was a two-and-a-half-ton army truck, "borrowed" for the evening.[62]

For every Jewish chaplain, the challenges were unique. Rabbis Robert S. Marcus and Herschel Schacter were involved with the transporting of children survivors from Buchenwald, Bergen-Belsen, and other concentration camps to relief settlements in Paris and Switzerland. From there, they were transported to Israel (then Palestine), their ultimate destination. These rabbis in uniform met and conducted negotiations with French and Swiss government officials, relief agencies, army representatives, and groups from Israel to help these orphans.

The chaplains felt acutely the pain and suffering of the survivors. Many of the victims were already quite ill and later died. The basic human needs for food, shelter, and clothing were almost impossible to obtain. Chaplain Max Braude gave insights into the determination of the rabbis to help obtain these supplies: "Daily we find more and more of the remnant of Israel and daily we continue to fight against great odds. We beg, we borrow, we cajole, we cuss and we get the stuff that is needed. . . . The task is mammoth but not hopeless and slowly we keep things going until this transition period is past."[63]

If there was any one rabbi who gave his all and risked his career to take care of the survivors, it was Rabbi Abraham Klausner. His accomplishments were extraordinary and affected the lives of thousands of Jews. Klausner arrived in Dachau in May 1945 with the 116th Evacuation Hospital Unit. While there, he began a program of reuniting victims with surviving family members. He concluded that a need existed to compile and publish volumes containing systematic lists of survivors. These books would then be distributed throughout the world, helping separated families reunite and learn the fate of lost family members.[64] Before he could put this plan into motion, his unit was ordered out of Dachau and sent to a resort area a hundred miles away. Klausner accompanied his unit to the rest area, but returned immediately to Dachau, telling the army that he had been reassigned there.

Klausner's tenacity and compassion for the survivors were intense.

In a recent interview he explained how the U.S. military had always assumed that all the survivors would want to return to their indigenous lands. Little thought or alternative planning had been allowed for Jews who had no desire to return to Germany, Poland, or Russia. He cites one instance when he came across a group of twelve hundred frightened concentration camp survivors, under the care of General Patton's Third Army, being told that they had to march with other survivors to a common displaced person's camp. This camp held, among others, Poles who had come to Germany to work during the war, making it hardly an acceptable place for Polish Jewish survivors. Chaplain Klausner, who was a lieutenant, intervened and told the Jews that they did not have to march anywhere. He then convinced the officer in charge that these Jews should not be forced to march. The next day, Klausner was ordered into Third Army Headquarters and placed in an office, where three colonels proceeded to scream at him. They asked him what authority he possessed to intervene and halt the transportation of the displaced persons. Klausner's position was that the individuals in question should be treated as Jews, not Poles or any other nationality. Klausner eventually won the argument, and the Jews were not forcibly marched anywhere and were housed in a separate camp.[65]

Rabbi Klausner was quick to point out that all of his accomplishments were achieved with the knowledge and assistance of military people. He operated for years with the support of other military rabbis, Christian chaplains, high-ranking officers, and enlisted people who believed in his cause. Klausner emphasized that it was only with the active support of the military structure that he was able to do this vast work. Whether with food, clothes, passports, transportation, medical attention, mail delivery, or the printing of books, Klausner had help, most of which came from within the military.[66]

Within a month, he had published his first volume of survivor names. Ultimately, he published six volumes, which were requested by relief agencies, organizations, and individuals from around the world. In addition to the lists of names, each volume contained information about the rights of the victims. Included among these rights was the ability to communicate with family and friends throughout the world. Since no mail service was available, Klausner urged survivors to give their letters to camp leaders, who in turn gave them to him. He used the military mail system to send these letters. Many rabbis resorted to this system. They communicated about needs for food, clothing, or medicine in letters sent back home, and soon boxes of collected materials were being sent directly to them for redistribution among the survivors.

The next project Klausner undertook was quite extensive. Building on his earlier success, he worked to ensure that Jewish displaced persons and those who required hospitalization were always kept in separate relief camps. Until then, Jewish refugees had been confined with other nationalities, which were often hostile to them. Such joint confinement created mistreatment, anxiety, and animosities. Jews in the local hospital, too, were traumatized by being treated by German doctors. Working with army officials and taking charge of local facilities, Klausner and others were able to establish a separate medical care system for these victims.[67]

In a letter sent to the CANRA, Rabbi Klausner expressed the feelings that motivated all of his efforts:

> Six weeks ago they were liberated. They were taken to a series of camps in the uniform of the Concentration camp and remained garbed in that infamous outfit. They are housed in dwellings that are unfit for human occupation and are fed in many cases less than they received at the Concentration camps. I do not use these words recklessly. I have traveled this entire area [Bavaria]. I have visited with each of the camps. [I have] spoken with the leaders, observed their mode of life and I turned aside in the best situation and silently cried—for all of Israel's sufferings, this! There seems to be no policy, no responsibility, no plan for these . . . stateless Jews.[68]

In addition to the immediate, lifesaving work he performed, Klausner also helped influence America policy toward Jewish survivors. Based on published reports about Jewish Holocaust victims and the difficulties they were encountering, President Truman in May 1945 appointed Earl G. Harrison, a former U.S. commissioner of immigration, to conduct an investigation. Harrison's mandate was clear: "to inquire into the needs of stateless and non-repatriable refugees among the displaced persons in Germany and to determine the extent to which those needs are now being met by military, governmental, and private organizations."[69]

Upon arriving in Germany, Harrison met with relief and military officials, including Chaplain Klausner. Klausner relates that his attendance at an initial meeting with Harrison was set up by an Army colonel from another command who wanted Klausner to be part of Harrison's entourage.[70] Harrison invited the chaplain to take part in his visit. For the next two months, they traveled throughout Germany and Austria, visiting camps, interviewing survivors, and experiencing firsthand the living conditions. Klausner's presence at Harrison's side helped shape his thinking about the refugees. Rabbi Klausner's perspectives about the clothing, feeding, special needs, and unique problems of Jewish survivors were appreciated and articulated by Harrison. In his final report he reaffirmed many of Klausner's ideas: "The first and plainest need of these people is a recognition of their actual status and by this I mean their status as Jews. . . . refusal to recognize the Jews as such has the effect, in this situation, of closing one's eyes to their former and more barbaric persecution, which has already made them a separate group with greater needs."[71]

Based on Harrison's report, President Truman directed the army to examine how it dealt with Jewish displaced persons. Among the many changes made as a result of the President's direction was the appointment of a Jewish chaplain, who reported to General Eisenhower. In August 1945 Rabbi Judah Nadich was ordered into the newly created position of "Advisor to the Commanding General on Jewish Affairs." General Eisenhower promulgated new regulations for Jewish refugees. One rule allowed for special camps to be established for Jewish victims who refused to return to their countries of origin. Chaplain Nadich's task involved traveling from camp to camp to ensure that U.S. military commanders adhered to these new regulations. Working directly on General Eisenhower's staff allowed Chaplain Nadich to correct many of the problems he had uncovered. He also acted as a coordinator between military authorities, German civilians, United Nations representatives, Joint Distribution Committee workers, and other relief agencies as they attempted to care for these survivors.[72]

In some cases, Rabbi Nadich encountered prejudice from high-

Above: Group of
concentration camp
survivors on the outskirts of
Munich, Germany. All
received aid and sustenance
from Chaplain Abraham
Klausner. Courtesy Mr. Abe
Plotkin.

Right: Corporal Abe Plotkin
(left) with Chaplain
Abraham Klausner. Courtesy
Mr. Abe Plotkin.

ranking military officers. Prominent among these individuals was General George S. Patton. Ignoring military instructions concerning the treatment of Holocaust survivors, Patton stated that Jews were "worse than animals . . . a subhuman species without any of the cultural or social refinements of our time."[73] This type of thinking and the blatant disregard of directives signed by General Eisenhower led to Patton's dismissal from service.

In spite of such blatant prejudices and the almost impossible tasks they faced, a relatively small number of Jewish chaplains had a substantial and heroic impact on the lives of these victims. It was, appropriately, Rabbi Klausner who received perhaps the most meaningful praise for the work he did, and it came from a survivor: "But, during these months in which Rabbi Klausner has been with us, he has so woven into our life that we see him as one of us. It is he who delights on our delight and suffers for our pains. It is he who understood his duty . . . at present we will not thank him, we say only—Rabbi, friend, brother, you have become one of us."[74]

With the conclusion of the war, most of the rabbis quickly returned to the civilian vocations of pulpit work, educational pursuits, and other aspects of the rabbinate. A few chose to work for the Veterans Administration, while a very few remained in the military and made that their life's work.

In this conflict, rabbis, guided by a sophisticated Jewish Welfare Board organization, achieved an inestimable number of accomplishments. In the midst of a society filled with anti-Semitic tendencies, they provided ministries to their personnel and thousands of others. They covered vast distances and counseled innumerable soldiers, sailors and marines of all faiths. They literally saved the lives of thousands of Holocaust survivors and gave them new hope for life. They preserved and prevailed, some giving their lives for the cause of freedom. The over three hundred rabbis who answered the call to serve their country made an indelible mark on the history of the chaplaincy and their country.

7

Adapting to a Changing World

In the decades between 1945 and the present, the world has experienced continued warfare. Wars in Korea and Vietnam and the conflict known as Desert Storm have become known to entire generations of Americans. In each of these conflicts, the United States armed forces, accompanied as always by clergy in uniform, played significant roles. This period brought a constitutional challenge to the chaplaincy and new assignments for military rabbis. Many "firsts" have occurred as well. The first female Jewish chaplain and the first rabbinic couple came into the military. Also, for the first time, services for Jewish members of the armed forces were held in Somalia, Saudi Arabia, Kuwait, and Bosnia.

In the years following the Second World War, nations that had been allies in the battle against Nazism rapidly became antagonists. Around the globe, Communist governments and interests were being forcibly advanced. With the onset of the Cold War, America became obsessed with ferreting out and acting against all forms of Communism. In Korea, divided at the thirty-eighth parallel, the situation was ripe for a confrontation. The southern half, helped by America, developed democratic institutions and initiated free elections, while the northern part, led by the Soviets, initiated a totalitarian regime. Armed forces on both sides grew.

On July 5, 1950, North Korean troops invaded South Korea and attacked South Korean and American forces. Within months, Chinese Communist forces crossed the border and joined forces with the North Koreans. The power of the Chinese attack surprised the South Korean and U.S. armies, and many soldiers died or became prisoners of war. These individuals received brutal treatment from the North Koreans and Chinese. Over thirty-three thousand Americans died in the three years of fighting, until the war's armistice in July 1953.[1]

During this time, military clergy experienced war in all its settings. Army and navy chaplains lived and ministered on frozen mountain-sides, in muddy trenches, with the wounded in aid stations, with re-treating troops, and under the harshest of conditions in prisoner-of-war camps. The brutal reality of this war has perhaps been best described by Chaplain Allen Newman. As part of his ministry, he carried stretchers to rescue soldiers wounded in battle:

> There in a shallow trench were the men who had been waiting for hours for us to come and get them. They were all seriously wounded. We had to decide which ones we could take and which ones would be left to the next trip. A decision like that might mean the difference between life and death for some of them. . . . Broken legs, missing legs, torn bodies, dirty wounds, all were common to those who depended upon our skill and judgement for some chance to live.[2]

Performing this type of service was commonplace for the chaplains.

As in prior conflicts, the Jewish community responded to the Korean crisis. In the years after the Second World War, new developments occurred, affecting the Jewish Welfare Board. In 1947 the Committee on Army and Navy Activities (CANRA) became reorganized as the Division of Religious Affairs, which in later years would be renamed again, becoming the Commission on Jewish Chaplaincy. The JWB as a whole underwent a major transformation, too. After an extensive study, it determined that its primary mission should be to facilitate the new and growing movement of Jewish community centers, not only to assist military members and their families.[3]

Most rabbis had returned home at the conclusion of the Second World War, and by the onset of the Korean fighting, only some thirty rabbis remained on active duty. To respond to the immediate need for Jewish chaplains, the three major rabbinical movements, through their seminaries—Yeshiva University (Orthodox), the Jewish Theological Seminary (Conservative), and Hebrew Union College's Jewish Institute of Religion (Reform)—imposed a voluntary draft system on their eligible rabbis. Each of the movements agreed to provide an equal num-

Chaplain Elihu Rickel sharing some good news with a young marine serving in Korea (maybe the birth of a baby!). Courtesy Marcus Center, American Jewish Archives.

Chaplain Rickel helping with a marine wounded in Korean battle. Courtesy Marcus Center, American Jewish Archives.

Chaplain Sam Sobel leading Jewish services aboard ship for troops heading into battle, September 1951. Courtesy Jewish Welfare Board Archives.

ber of rabbis for a two-year period of service.[4] Through this process, a total of one hundred rabbis came on active duty by 1953.

Over the course of the Korean War, rabbis provided the same hands-on ministry described above. Twelve received the Bronze Star for heroic actions, and one, Samuel Sobel, was also awarded the Purple Heart for having been wounded in battle. The citation written for Rabbi Sobel detailed his efforts: "Carrying out frequent trips to the front line, he imparted strength and peace of mind to the troops throughout many days and nights while under heavy enemy artillery and mortar fire. . . . He ministered to the spiritual needs of the wounded and dying at the front lines, forward aid stations and medical companies of the division."[5] As a navy chaplain assigned to the marines, Rabbi Sobel recounted that his fellow chaplains utilized the same jeep when visiting the troops. They painted a sign on the vehicle that

Chaplain Oscar Lifshutz chats with troops celebrating Passover in Seoul, Korea, 1950. Courtesy Jewish Welfare Board Archives.

read "Marine Padres Incorporated."[6] A cross and a Star of David adorned each side of the sign. This demonstration of pluralism and mutual respect must have been a positive role model for the troops.

Major holidays, such as Passover, created opportunities to bring together Jewish soldiers, who for the most part prayed individually or in small groups. During Passover 1952, Chaplain Herbert Brichto initiated a program titled "Operation Matzo." This project involved planning, obtaining supplies, and figuring out logistics for a major seder observance. He found a damaged Korean schoolhouse large enough to hold the expected number of participants. With funds supplied by the Jewish Welfare Board, he hired Korean laborers to assist with the cleaning and refurbishing of the building. Army Engineers ensured adequate supplies of water and electrical power. By the night of the seder, almost one thousand troops had arrived from Seoul for the special occasion. In addition to U.S. forces, military personnel from Britain, Canada,

A field service held for Rosh Hashanah (the Jewish New Year) by Chaplain Murray Rothman, Korea, 1953. Courtesy Jewish Welfare Board Archives.

Soldiers at prayer, September 1952, Korea. Courtesy Jewish Welfare Board Archives.

Luxemburg, Israel, Turkey, and Greece participated. High-ranking officers gave speeches about freedom, and members of families fighting in different military units were reunited at the seder. Brothers met brothers, and uncles met nephews. Chaplain Brichto described the event:

> "Operation Matzo" was indeed a mammoth success. For three glorious days away from the war, it provided one thousand men with food, lodging, religious services, recreational facilities, gifts and comfort items. Even the weather was beautiful. It was not until the last of our guests had departed, carrying boxes of matzo, and cans of gefilte fish and kosher beef back to the front, that the spring rains came.[7]

Passover 1953 found six rabbis working to ensure that the Jewish troops received and ate kosher-for-Passover food items. The rabbis, representing army, navy, and marine commands, formed what they labeled "Operation Third Passover in Korea." This group gathered all available supplies, divided them up among themselves, and then headed back to their various camps and bases to officiate at Passover services and festive meals. Six mud-covered jeeps carried supplies to troops. The name on each jeep, stenciled for the occasion on its front and rear, said much about both its occupant and the morale of the troops. Names such as "The Rough Riding Rabbi," "Rabbi From Brooklyn," the "Shema Yisroel," (Hear O Israel), and "Red Sea Special" inspired and attracted the attention of all Jewish personnel, informing them that Passover was coming and that their spiritual and dietary needs would be met.[8]

Despite such valiant attempts to maintain morale, the chaplains' ministry in Korea became increasingly difficult as negotiations to end the war dragged on, seemingly without end. During the years of peace talks, fighting continued, casualties rose, and morale declined. Through it all, the Jewish chaplains held weekly sabbath and holiday services, maintained communications, and ministered to their troops.

As the peace talks were commencing in Korea, the French were fighting in Vietnam. Vietnam had two distinct republics, divided at the seventeenth parallel. The Democratic Republic of Vietnam in the North, supported by the Soviet Union and the Chinese, opposed the Republic of Vietnam, backed by the French and the United States government. American forces began training the South Vietnamese army.[9] America's determination to fight Communism was evidenced by the establishment, in February 1962, of the U.S. Military Command, Vietnam (MACV). The country slid once again into a brutal war. In the words of Rodger Venzke, "In fact, there are no beachheads to storm, no conventional invasions to repel, no discernible front lines of combat, and no easily identified enemy. Silently, slowly at first, through the complicated course of international politics, American soldiers found themselves in a strange land and a bitter conflict."[10]

Because of Congressional support, such as the 1964 Gulf of Tonkin Resolution, American troops arrived in record numbers in Vietnam. By the end of 1966, almost four hundred thousand troops had arrived, and combat deaths rose to over six thousand. The number of chaplains grew in proportion to the rapid growth of troops. The chaplain's ministry in Vietnam was especially dangerous. Many chaplains utilized helicopters to visit their troops in remote jungle posts and camps. Booby traps, ambushes, friendly fire, stealthy Viet-Cong, and night attacks were everpresent dangers. Navy Chaplain Edwin V. Bohula served with the marines and offered this description of a typical operation:

> My luck was to have our copter land in the middle of a rice paddy and as I jumped out I went waist deep in the muck. The first minute in the field on a new operation and I smelled "like that" again. We walked and climbed over hills. Snipers worked us over but prisoners, weapons and supplies were taken. . . . Leeches were all over us from the paddies. The rains came at this point as on the other operations, and we were wet day and night.[11]

Vietnam was a bloody war. Some chaplains risked or lost their lives while attempting to carry or drag the wounded to safety. In a noteworthy rescue effort in September 1967, Father Vincent R. Capodanno became the first navy chaplain killed in Vietnam. His company of marines came in close contact with enemy troops, and fighting ensued. Under fire, Chaplain Capodanno ministered to wounded marines. In his final act, he placed his body between an enemy gunner and a badly wounded soldier and began bandaging the soldier's wounds. Within moments he had been fatally wounded by the enemy gunner. Chaplain

Capodanno's efforts have become legendary in the Chaplain Corps and serve as an inspiring model for future spiritual leaders.[12]

Another significant role of the chaplain was to help young troops deal with all of the emotions associated with battle situations. As the war progressed and its unpopularity grew, chaplains increasingly became involved in other issues as well. They counseled personnel who abused drugs, promoted racism, or began to mistrust the military. In whatever circumstances, from counseling to caring for the wounded, chaplains were always totally concerned about their people.

The number of rabbis serving in Vietnam at any one time was limited. From 1965, when only one army rabbi served there, until the height of the United States involvement in Vietnam, four army rabbis and a smaller number of navy rabbis met the needs of Jewish personnel. These rabbis covered great distances to maintain contact with their congregations. Generally, chaplains visited outlying bases regularly, focusing on conducting sabbath services, providing religious education and counseling, and distributing religious items.

Often these trips involved risks. Chaplain Mark A. Abramowitz described a typical sabbath service held for army and air force personnel at Da Nang Air Base: "It was inevitably Friday nights when rocket attacks took place and usually during our services. Much of the service was held on the floor as we talked about those pilots who were flying sorties at that exact time and what the others felt about it."[13] This was typical of the risk experienced by most rabbis in Vietnam.

The rabbis received enormous support for their ministry from the stateside Jewish communities. In the fall of 1966, Rabbi E. David Lapp, an army chaplain in Vietnam, organized a massive celebration for Hanukkah. Parents, wives, and girlfriends of Jewish personnel tape-recorded messages called "Living Letters." Additionally, the JWB's Women's Organization Services across the country collected and shipped holiday treats to Vietnam. With air force help, Rabbi Lapp distributed the recordings and holiday items in an effort he called "Operation Maccabee." His area of coverage included thirty thousand square miles, with over seven hundred Jewish personnel.[14]

In addition to receiving help from home, rabbi chaplains had many interesting cross-cultural experiences in Vietnam. Rabbi Lapp, for in-

Chaplain E. David Lapp leading prayer service circa 1967, Vietnam. Courtesy Jewish Welfare Board Archives.

stance, reported to the Jewish Welfare Board that, during his tour in Vietnam, he presented a lecture to Vietnamese students at the Nha Trang Theological Seminary. His lectures, as well as his responses to questions, were translated from English to Vietnamese and back.[15]

As in every war in which they were involved, rabbis faced challenges in Vietnam related to performing religious services. Passover observances held in April 1967 accurately reflected the tasks of rabbis in Vietnam. Three Jewish chaplains—E. David Lapp, David B. Saltzman, and Alan M. Greenspan—divided the country into thirds. Each became responsible for publicizing the location and time of Passover services and meals in his geographical area. Passover seders were always well attended, as they provided comfort to troops far away from home. And as in other wars, even the seder, with all its unique traditions, became different in Vietnam.

> There was a new item on the Sedar plate this year. A Malaria pill. It
> was Monday—Malaria pill day. This was Passover in Vietnam. . . . No

Chaplain Robert L. Reiner leading services on a hilltop in Da Nang, Vietnam. *(Left to right):* Private First Class Shaw, Captain Schiffer, Rabbi Reiner. Courtesy Jewish Welfare Board Archives.

one wore a tie and a few wore civilian clothes. Some wore the same soiled clothes that had been in combat near Pleiku, Bong Son or Tuy Hoa the day before. . . . The Seder had to be abbreviated, because there was a curfew in Nha Trang and the troops had to be returned to their billets shortly. . . . Most of the troops felt the inspiration of the moment, especially when the chaplain intoned, And we look forward to the day when we will be able to return to Israel. One GI added, And to the United States. This was Passover in Vietnam.[16]

Such get-togethers boosted morale and helped the troops overcome feelings of isolation.

Another major role played by military rabbis was that of training, educating, and communicating with Jewish lay leaders. Lay leaders served as points of contact between the rabbis and the individual units

Kosher kitchen maintained by Chaplain Breslau for Jewish service-men in Phu Bai, Vietnam, 1968. Rabbi Breslau, far right. Courtesy Jewish Welfare Board Archives.

Passover seder, Nha Trang, Vietnam, 1969. Courtesy Jewish Welfare Board Archives.

and ships in Vietnam. Their task, always done in a voluntary capacity, included identifying Jewish personnel and keeping them informed about services, social events, or rabbinical visits. In many places, lay leaders held religious services in the chaplains' absence. Military rabbis distributed newsletters entitled *The Saigon South Shalom* and *The Vietnam Jewish Chronicle* as another form of maintaining contact with a very widely dispersed group of troops.

Two of these hardworking rabbis died during active services in Vietnam. Rabbi Meir Engel was the first Jewish chaplain in Vietnam, arriving there in August 1964. In December of that year, at the age of fifty, he passed away of a heart attack. Rabbi Morton H. Singer had been in Vietnam for only six weeks in 1968 when he and fourteen others died in an Air Force transport plane tragedy.[17]

For many, Vietnam left lasting impressions. As Rabbi Marc A. Golub completed his tour of Vietnam, he wrote the following:

> As I boarded the aircraft, I hoped that I had contributed something to the men that I had served, that my all even though what I had given was surely far less that *[sic]* what those who had lost their lives or had left behind. As I too[k] one last look back at the dirty, steaming, warridden land, I remembered the line attributed to Jacob in the Tora, "Surely God has been in this place and I do not know it." I wondered if God really had been here and if I had properly recognized his presence. Only God knew. Only He could bring peace when men abandon it. Vietnam was over for me—a happening, a memory, a chapter in my life, now closed.[18]

Within a few years after the conclusion of the Vietnam War, the legality of the military chaplaincy came under scrutiny. In November 1979, Joel Katcoff and Allen M. Weider, two seniors at Harvard University Law School, filed a civil lawsuit in the U.S. District Court of Brooklyn, New York. Their main legal argument suggested that the army chaplaincy violated the establishment clause of the First Amendment to the Constitution, "Congress shall make no law respecting an establishment of religion or prohibiting the free exercise thereof."[19]

Over the next six years these men pursued this case. They initially demanded, unsuccessfully, that the court issue an injunction restrain-

Chaplain Meir Engel leading sabbath services, November 23, 1963. Fort Ord, California. Courtesy Jewish Welfare Board Archives.

ing the government from spending any more funds to support the military chaplaincy. The law students maintained that privately funded, civilian chaplaincy programs could meet the needs of armed forces personnel. Their complaint filled eleven legal-sized pages and included an additional section containing over 123 further interrogatories seeking information about army chaplaincy practices.[20]

Three governmental groups responded to this case. To help coordinate these efforts, the army recalled to active duty Rabbi Israel Drazin, a reserve chaplain (colonel) and practicing attorney. For his work on this case, Chaplain Drazin was promoted to Brigadier General. Rabbi Drazin focused on the issue of the free exercise of religion for soldiers as the primary defense for the chaplaincy. He recommended consistently that chaplains be knowledgeable of and act in accordance with this principle. This approach stressed that military chaplains helped all armed forces personnel meet their religious needs, regardless of the chaplain's specific religion. On January 22, 1985, the Second Circuit Court rendered its decision affirming the constitutionality of the army chaplaincy. The judges noted that Congress had authorized the chaplaincy in 1791. They further found that soldiers were entitled to the free exercise of religion wherever they were in the world, and that military chaplains provided them with this and other forms of counseling and education.[21]

Other recent changes include an alteration of insignia; in 1982 the military insignia worn by Jewish chaplains was modified. The Roman numerals previously used to represent the Ten Commandments were replaced with the first ten letters of the Hebrew alphabet. This change had been supported by a number of active-duty and reserve rabbis.

The influence and significance of the reserve rabbis in helping maintain a Jewish presence in the military cannot be overestimated. Many prominent rabbis, such as Barry H. Greene, Herschel Schacter, and Matthew Simon, served on active duty for years and then remained in the military reserves. At the same time, they pursued active and highly successful careers in the civilian rabbinate. These rabbis and others who followed similar career patterns formed a powerful cadre of individuals who represented their prospective rabbinical movements and continually assisted the growth of the Jewish chaplaincy.

Some rabbis, such as Aaron Landes, were selected to be chief of chaplains for all naval reserve chaplains. In 1987, Rear Admiral Landes followed in the footsteps of a fellow rabbi from Pennsylvania, Rabbi Bertram Korn, a prominent rabbi, author, and congregational rabbi who had received the rank of rear admiral in 1975. Rabbi Landes served two years on active duty and thirty-two years in the reserves. During this time he had an enormous influence on the chaplaincy as a whole, its rabbis, and the Jewish community. To give a small indication of his activities, he helped initiate a Jewish chapel at the U.S. Naval Academy and then persuaded the navy to assign a full-time rabbi there.

Wherever troops went, their chaplains followed. In 1983 U.S. forces were sent to Beirut, Lebanon, as part of an international peacekeeping effort. In October, tragedy struck when a suicidal bomber drove a vehicle under a building housing U.S. Marines and detonated a massive explosion, killing hundreds. Navy chaplains Arnold Resnicoff and George Pucciarelli, a rabbi and a Catholic priest, had been visiting with the troops the previous night and were quartered a few hundred feet from the initial blast. Chaplain Resnicoff's account of that time offers a quintessential picture of the work of a chaplain and the interfaith cooperation he upheld:

> Working with the wounded—sometimes comforting, and simply letting them know help was on the way; sometimes trying to pull and carry those whose injuries appeared less dangerous in an immediate sense than the approaching fire or the smothering smoke—my *kippa* [skullcap] was lost. The last I remember it, I had used it to wipe someone's brow. Father Pucciarelli, the Catholic chaplain, cut a circle out of his cap, a piece of camouflage cloth that would become my temporary covering. . . . Somehow, we both wanted to shout the message in a land where people were killing each other, at least partially based on the differences in religion among them, that *we*—we Americans—still believed that we could be proud of our particular religions and yet work side by side when the time came to help others, to comfort, and to ease pain.[22]

This working relationship among faith groups in times of peace and of crisis also existed within the JWB. In the early 1980s, the JWB's Commission on Jewish Chaplaincy (CJC), representing, as always, the major branches of Judaism, reached consensus on several issues affecting military rabbis. These included agreements not to officiate at mixed marriages (1981) and not to solicit converts to Judaism (1983), the creation of a new prayer book acceptable to all Jewish personnel (1984), and a unified CJC policy for the Department of Defense concerning the wearing of the yarmulke (skullcap), sabbath observances, beards, and kashrut (kosher food).[23] However, in the summer of 1985, an issue arose that presented unique challenges to the JWB's principle of accommodation and consensus-building.

In the summer of 1985, student Rabbi Julie Schwartz and her husband, Steven Ballaban, also a rabbinic student at the Hebrew Union College's Jewish Institute of Religion, decided to enter the navy as chaplains. Schwartz became the first female rabbi chaplain, and they

Chaplain Arnold Resnicoff with his camouflage yarmulke (skullcap) after the Beirut, Lebanon, explosion. Courtesy Jewish Welfare Board Archives.

became the first rabbinic chaplain couple. Initially, Rabbi Schwartz thought that she would be a reservist, following in the footsteps of Rabbi Bonnie Koppell, a Reconstructionist rabbi whom the JWB-CJC had endorsed in 1979 to serve in the army chaplaincy as a reservist. However, after attending the navy chaplain's basic training course in the summer of 1985, both Rabbis Schwartz and Ballaban decided to request endorsement for active duty. This decision initiated a crisis for the status quo of the JWB-CJC. They had no problem with Rabbi Ballaban, but Rabbi Schwartz's desire for the JWB's imprimatur created a dilemma.

Previously all candidates for the chaplaincy had been interviewed and approved by rabbis representing all the rabbinic movements, an act of cooperation with a value that cannot be overestimated. As mentioned, the new armed forces prayer book, written in 1984, had been produced by a committee of rabbis from all three Jewish movements.

Veterans Administration Chaplain David Spitz and Cantor Burt Allen provide services for the Jewish veterans in the Chicago area, circa 1990. Courtesy Jewish Welfare Board Archives.

But because of the need for a consensus, much thought and energy went into the deliberations about the endorsement of Rabbi Schwartz. In this case, consensus proved to be impossible.

The Reform movement in 1972 had ordained its first female rabbi; the Conservative movement followed in 1985. Their representatives to the JWB-CJC felt that a female chaplain should be endorsed as a matter of course. But the Rabbinical Council of America, representing the Orthodox branch of Judaism, did not and does not accept the validity of a female functioning as a rabbi. Its representative on the CJC would therefore not endorse her for the chaplaincy. Even an abstention was unacceptable. This issue received much press attention in the secular and Jewish press. By May 1986, Rabbi Schwartz had still not received her endorsement from the JWB, without which she would be unable to come on active duty.

In the widely publicized May meeting of the JWB-CJC the Central Conference of American Rabbis, the Reform rabbinical organization, announced its intention to endorse Rabbi Schwartz unilaterally for the chaplaincy. Based on this precedent, each separate rabbinic movement now held the right to certify its own candidates for the chaplaincy. The immediate effect of this independent action was the resignation of the Orthodox contingent of the Commission on Jewish Chaplaincy, since it could not be associated with the endorsement of a female rabbi as a military chaplain.

Yet the dissolution of the JWB Commission on Jewish Chaplaincy was brief. Within moments, a new cooperative entity was created, the JWB Jewish Chaplains Council. Future endorsements of chaplains for the military would be done by each constituent rabbinic group, while the council would process the endorsements and forward them to Washington. The JWB Jewish Chaplains Council continues to serve as the representative body for all Jewish endorsements for the military and Veterans Administration chaplaincy.

Rabbi Schwartz and her husband served successful tours of duty in the navy. Due to Chaplain Schwartz's tenacity and the support provided by many rabbis, she paved the way for other women to follow. She described her experiences in this historic role:

> I was never a "first" in anything until this happened. Now I understand why the first women who open doors can be angry and bitter. It's very hard being a first—people are constantly watching me to make sure I don't slip up. As the navy's only female Jewish chaplain, I feel that every time I do something it has to be especially good. At the same time, I have to be one of the boys because I'm surrounded by men.[24]

While the issue of endorsing Rabbi Schwartz generated a great deal of publicity, other issues concerning Jews in the military were unfolding.

In March 1986 the Supreme Court held, in a 5-to-4 vote, that a military ban on the wearing of religious headgear was constitutional. The case involved an air force psychologist, S. Simcha Goldman, who wore his yarmulke (skullcap) during his daily work at an air force base's mental health clinic. When ordered to remove his yarmulke, even though he had previously worn it on active duty, Goldman, who was also an ordained rabbi, refused. This decision prompted air force disciplinary actions. Dr. Goldman initiated a legal suit against the government, alleging that his First Amendment rights of freedom of religion were being denied. The court's decision set in motion a number of initiatives in the Congress. Within a year, legislation known as the "yarmulke amendment" passed through Congress; it stipulated that "neat and conservative" religious apparel that did not interfere with the performance of a member's military responsibilities were acceptable.[25]

While these legal issues were being resolved, new programs were developed that benefited Jewish and non-Jewish personnel. In 1987 Chaplain Norman Auerback became the first full-time rabbi assigned to the United States Naval Academy. Prior to his arrival, Jewish midshipmen had worshiped at local synagogues. Rabbi Auerback created programs that benefited the entire brigade of midshipmen. One of his accomplishments was to bring a renewed emphasis to the observance of the Days of Holocaust Remembrance. In April 1989 Auerback developed an impressive Holocaust observance. Along with academy Jewish lay leaders, he acquired Torah scrolls rescued from the Holocaust. At the conclusion of the program, the Torahs were carried through the academy grounds to the Jewish chapel, where they remain on permanent display.[26] Rabbi Albert I. Slomovitz followed Auerback at the Academy and initiated interfaith awareness lectures and trips to Israel.

Another international conflict arose in August 1990 when Iraq invaded Kuwait. The United States formed a coalition with a number of countries and, under the aegis of the United Nations, developed a strategy for retaking Kuwait. As the U.S. armed forces organized for war, chaplains, both active and reserve, prepared to serve in their traditional roles as spiritual mentors in the Persian Gulf. Jewish chaplains, for the first time, were called upon to be present in Kuwait, Saudi Arabia, and Iraq.

Chaplain Ben Romer was the first active-duty rabbi involved in this conflict and the last to leave. He arrived in Saudi Arabia near the end of August 1990 and served almost nine months before returning home.

Chaplain Norman Auerback leads procession with Holocaust Torah scrolls through United States Naval Academy, April 1989. Courtesy Jewish Welfare Board Archives.

Romer, a veteran of the Panama Campaign, was attached to the 724th Infantry Regiment, a part of the Twenty-fourth Infantry Division based at Fort Stewart in Georgia. Romer's military congregation grew daily as thousands of new troops arrived in the country. His primary task involved identifying Jewish lay leaders spread out over large geographical areas and organizing them into effective points of contact for Jewish personnel.

Rabbi Romer quickly realized that travel in Saudi Arabia brought unique challenges. He had to contend with desert sandstorms and temperatures of over 130 degrees. Often, as in Vietnam, military helicopters proved to be the only practical way of visiting troops spread over wide areas.

In November and December 1990, Chaplain Romer reported to the JWB Jewish Chaplains Council that he had identified between three

Above: Ministry to troops means being with them: Chaplain Albert I. Slomovitz joining midshipmen at the United States Naval Academy for a morning workout, July 1991.

Right: Meals at the academy also provided opportunities for counseling. Chaplain Albert I. Slomovitz talking with a new midshipman, July 1991.

hundred and five hundred Jewish troops. For Hanukkah, Romer traveled from camp to camp, conducting sabbath and holiday services and distributing mail, cards, and gifts addressed to "Any Jewish Solider."[27] Eventually, other military rabbis joined Rabbi Romer; however, for the first four months of the Gulf War, he single-handedly maintained the Jewish presence in the entire operational land area and provided religious support to his troops as well.

While Chaplain Romer provided coverage on the ground, Jewish sailors and marines at sea received religious support from navy rabbis. Chaplain Maurice Kaprow served aboard the aircraft carrier USS *Saratoga*. As the need arose, Rabbi Kaprow traveled by helicopter to other ships in the vicinity, conducting services and counseling personnel. This process involved an unusual form of transportation via a helicopter that was known to many as the "Holy Helo." Since many of the smaller ships did not have facilities for the landing of a helicopter, the rabbi was hooked to an electric winch and lowered to and from the deck of the ship. Rabbi Kaprow maintained a regular schedule of such visits: "I am a frequent flier on helicopters. . . . I fly once a week on the average, and see as many Jews as I can throughout the battle group. I do it because I can see the joy in their faces to have the chance to meet a rabbi in uniform."[28] Chaplain Kaprow's presence helped sustain Judaism in isolated and difficult circumstances.

One of the more intriguing stories about Jewish troops involved a Jewish lay leader, Army Captain Bill Peterson. Captain Peterson arrived in Saudi Arabia at around the same time as Chaplain Romer; however, Rabbi Romer's extensive ministry to combat units made it almost impossible to provide ongoing religious coverage for Captain Peterson's area. As a JWB-certified lay leader, Captain Peterson quickly gathered Jewish personnel in his area and, within a few weeks time and with other lay leaders, he conducted sabbath and holiday services. Information about this activity passed by word of mouth among the troops and via other military chaplains. At that time, due to a concern for Saudi sensitivities, religious services were designated as "C" for Catholic, "P" Protestant, or "J" Jewish and were referred to as morale activities. The chaplains were designated "Morale Officers."[29]

This lay-led group named itself Congregation Ivrei Hamidbar

Chaplain Maurice Kaprow utilizing the Holy Helo (short for Holy Helicopter) for getting from ship to ship to visit personnel, circa January 1991. Courtesy Jewish Welfare Board Archives.

ha'Aravi, "Hebrews of the Arabian Desert." Captain Peterson described the group's uniqueness as "J x 2." "We all were Jews (in an anti-Jewish land) and Joint (a term for all military branches: Army, Navy and Air Force)."[30] The religious practices followed by the group symbolized its diversity: "Our religious practices were guided by the eclectic practices of the Havurah movement. Coming from so many different communities across the spectrum of Jewish religious practice, we had to create our own traditions. In this, we blended the special moments each of us brought here from home to the enrichment of the whole group."[31] In March 1991 the group observed a special Purim. This holiday celebrates the defeat of Haman, an ancient Jewish adversary; the group added a modern foe, Saddam Hussein, who also suffered defeat. Lay leaders such as Captain Peterson, along with the congregation he and others led, provided opportunities for the expression of Jewish spirituality during the Gulf War.

In mid-December 1990, Chaplain (Lieutenant Colonel) David Zalis, an army reservist, arrived in Saudi Arabia. As the senior-ranking Jewish chaplain, he became their leader. He also served as the point of contact for many of the groups desirous of sending supplies to the troops. Chaplain Zalis, like Chaplain Romer, traveled extensively to visit Jewish personnel. Meeting with troops took on an increased significance as Desert Shield became Desert Storm in January 1991. On one of his trips through the desert, Rabbi Zalis related a story typical of military ministry:

> I found about 20 people waiting for a 1530 (3:30 PM) Protestant service. Torrential rains had delayed the chaplain, so I ended up conducting together with the Corps Sergeant Major, who is Protestant, and my assistant who is Catholic. This was three days before the war, and I spoke to them about Hashem [God] hardening the heart of Pharaoh, and what happened afterwards to him, drawing the obvious analogy to Saddam Hussein.[32]

Travel proved arduous and difficult during Rabbi Zalis's service in the Gulf. In one four-day period, Chaplain Zalis and his assistant drove 1600 miles, parked for the nights near Saudi police stations, and slept in their vehicle.

Chaplain David Zalis *(left)* greeting General Norman
Schwarzkopf, circa January 1991. Courtesy Jewish Welfare
Board Archives.

One main challenge of Rabbi Zalis's work was the procuring of
kosher food items for Jewish personnel. He also worked to acquire
kosher-for-Passover food items. Chaplain Zalis utilized three diverse
sources for these kosher food supplies. The first was the military: the
food services officer recognized the needs of some Jewish troops for
kosher food. Within two months, substantial amounts of kosher food
products had arrived for distribution. The JWB–Jewish Chaplains
Council provided a second source of supplies. The JWB arranged for
hundreds of individual boxes of Passover foods, known as solo-seder
kits, to be used for Passover.

The final source for kosher food was unusual. Two rabbinic colleagues of Rabbi Zalis's from New York began raising funds for food.
Kosher items were ordered from Guttman Catering in Zurich, Switzerland. Jewish lay leaders then picked up these supplies and transported them to Rhein-Main Air Force Base in Germany, where they

were forwarded to Riyadh. Chaplain Zalis received these items and distributed them to troops, lay leaders, and chaplains.[33]

The Passover seders organized by Rabbi Zalis proved to be historic. The military rented the cruise ship *Cunard Princess* as a rest-and-relaxation location for troops. The ship's location in Bahrain kept it away from military operations. Zalis realized that this represented an ideal venue for the coming year's Passover celebration, to be held from March 29 through the first of April. Beginning in January 1991, he began planning for this all-service-wide event. In March he received the official approval of Commanding General Norman Schwarzkopf to host the occasion.[34]

Fellow military chaplains played a crucial role in the publicizing the seder. In addition to notifying Jewish personnel, chaplains assisted with transportation to and from Bahrain and helped with other issues that might have prevented troops from attending. Chaplain (Colonel) Gaylord E. Hatler, the senior army chaplain, expressed his thoughts about the seder in a March 10, 1991, memorandum to other chaplains: "I need your help in ensuring that as many Jewish personnel as possible attend the Passover Seders. . . . your help in identifying Jewish personnel and getting your commander's permission for them for this retreat is essential."[35] This support ensured that over four hundred service personnel participated in the seder programs.

While the seder took place aboard the *Cunard Princess*, Rabbi Jon Cutler, a navy chaplain assigned with marines, held one in a different environment. His main area of coverage encompassed the Kuwait-Saudi border. In a jeep packed with kosher foods and religious supplies, he visited and counseled military members. During Passover in Kuwait, he led a unique seder. His recollection of the observance reflected the fact that the retreating Iraqis had set off numerous fires, which took months to extinguish: "I filled plastic cups with salt water . . . when I turned around there were oil droplets on the top of the salt water and dead flies in the wine. The oil was everywhere. That was very miserable."[36] After the seder meals, Cutler encountered a group of starving Kuwait children. He gave them boxes of Manischewitz matzoh and cans of matzoh-ball soup to carry home for their next meals.

One of the more intriguing experiences of the Gulf War occurred in Israel. There, Orthodox Rabbi Jacob Goldstein, a major in the New York National Guard, became the senior chaplain to American and Dutch soldiers sent to Israel to maintain the Patriot antimissile batteries used against Iraqi Scud rockets. His unofficial title was "Harav HaPatriots," "The Rabbi of the Patriots." In this role, he acted as a point of contact between his troops and their Israeli hosts. Despite the fact that only a small number of his troops were Jewish, Chaplain Goldstein took care of their spiritual needs. As he emphasized, "I call myself a religious officer, I happen to be Jewish on a personal level. My responsibility is to all my troops."[37]

From the Middle East to all parts of the globe, Jewish chaplains still operate in unusual circumstances. Navy Chaplain Mitchell Schranz served aboard the naval station in Subic Bay, Phillippines. During the summer of 1991, a dormant volcano became quite active. Mount Pinatubo erupted and covered a good portion of the island with volcanic ash, and the infrastructures of the air force and naval bases were destroyed. The military decided to evacuate the spouses and children of service members. Military ships and planes were pressed into service for this emergency evacuation. Chaplain Schranz's family was among those who left, all within a few days after the volcano had erupted and changed their lives. He remained behind and offered this description of his work:

> Father Bob Reidy, RP3 [Religious Program Specialist–Third Class] Tony Malacus and I delivered tons of food from damaged commissary warehouses. As time wore on, chaplains spearheaded ongoing humanitarian efforts to help people deal with the after-affects of Pinatubo. Ministries to our Sailors and Marines were geared to help them cope with stress, anxiety, and separation from loved ones. . . . it was, as Charles Dickens wrote: the best of times, the worst of times.[38]

From the Phillippines to Submarine Base Kings Bay Georgia, the ministry of military rabbis continues. In April 1994, I spent five days aboard the USS *Maryland*, a Trident-class nuclear submarine. I had come to the Kings Bay area to conduct a seder program that R. Bruce Pierce, a Protestant chaplain and a friend, had arranged and publi-

Rabbis Barry Greene and Matthew Simon *(left and right)* visit with Chaplain Jacob Goldstein in Israel, with Patriot missile batteries in the background, circa February 1991. Courtesy Jewish Welfare Board Archives.

cized.[39] I was asked then to spend five days on a submarine, a period that included Easter Sunday. Protestant and Catholic lay leaders conducted their holiday services on the submarine. The ship's officers made a special request for me to be a guest speaker on Easter Sunday morning.

I considered this an honor. That morning, I brought some matzoh with me, which was left over from Passover. In my talk with the crew, I spoke about matzoh and what it represented: God acting in history, the Exodus story of moving from slavery into freedom, and the feelings about home and family that these holidays brought to mind. At the conclusion of my talk, there was a period of silence and communal prayers for the ship's safety and the welfare of loved ones. The service concluded with everyone having a taste of matzoh. My sense of spirituality and purpose as a chaplain was reinforced. What a unique and uplifting service, held hundreds of feet below the Atlantic Ocean.

Currently I am the navy senior chaplain for the Pensacola, Florida, area. This position means that I and my staff are directly responsible for the spiritual well-being of about fifteen thousand active duty service people and their family members. My staff includes about twenty people: chaplains, navy petty officers and enlisted personnel, civilian staff, and chapel volunteers. Part of my job is to ensure that a Muslim prayer room being built as part of the chapel complex is properly dedicated and reverently maintained. Any issues regarding aspects of the Christian services or educational programs offered also come through me, as I am the senior chaplain. Of course I provide for the religious needs of Jewish personnel in this area, as well as on other bases in the southeast part of the country. Other military rabbis all around the world are in similar positions of leadership. From the end of the Second World War to the present, rabbis in uniform (fighting rabbis!) have remained in the armed forces, continuing their historical tasks of counseling, blessing, educating, and accompanying those who go in harm's way.

Rabbis in uniform, led by their rabbinical ancestors in the armed forces, are an established and recognized part of the U.S. military chaplaincy. In fact, more attention and publicity is placed now on the newer denominations and faith groups entering the spiritual ministry of the armed forces.

It is hoped that the data uncovered in this research can help the American-Jewish community put to rest cultural misunderstandings about the Jewish relationship with the military. Jews and their rabbis have always played an integral role in the defense of this country. The organized Jewish community has maintained a definite and significant function in this regard.

From the early days in New Amsterdam to the Civil War, it was the community that organized and fought for the legal and moral right for rabbis to serve as ministers in uniform. Prior to the First World War, in the midst of charges of Jews being unpatriotic, much communal attention was again focused on Jews in the military. This concern created the impetus for the development of the Jewish Welfare Board. The growth and accomplishments of this component of the American-Jewish community have been phenomenal. Representing almost the entire spectrum of American Judaism for both world wars, wars in Korea and Vietnam, and Desert Storm, this group recruited rabbis, trained welfare workers, supplied troops with religious articles, and met the spiritual needs of men and women heading into battle.

Ultimately, however, this book has been about rabbis and their deeds. These "Fighting Rabbis" included Elkan Voorsanger, Lee Levinger, Abraham Klausner, and many others who did unusual things in unbelievable circumstances. Some, such as the ninety rabbis who came in contact with the displaced persons of the Second World War, made a difference between life and death for countless individuals. Others, like Rabbi Alexander Goode, made the ultimate sacrifice of their lives for their nation.

The history of these unsung heroes continues through to the present. Male and female rabbis do their part in the military. From services in the desert of Kuwait to High Holiday services in Somalia and Bosnia, rabbis in uniform are present. As long as American-Jewish sons and daughters and their contemporaries are in uniform defending their country, rest assured that they will have rabbis next to them. May the Almighty watch over all who serve their country, their families and loved ones, and the rabbis who choose to go on this journey with them.

Appendix

Seeking God's Presence

Arnold E. Resnicoff

Navy Chaplain Arnold Resnicoff's account of the Beirut truck-bomb attack on October 23, 1983, was so well received that President Ronald Reagan used it as his keynote address to a 1984 Baptist convention chaired by the Reverend Jerry Falwell and attended by over twenty thousand ministers. This was the first time that a president had ever read a rabbi's report as his keynote address.

When I found myself staring at the horror of the truck bomb exploding that day in Beirut, there was an impulse to cry out that we had, indeed, been forsaken. One of the first to reach the building after the blast, I—along with Lieutenant Commander George ("Pooch") Pucciarelli, the Catholic chaplain attached to the marine unit—faced a scene almost too terrible to describe. Bodies, and pieces of bodies, were everywhere. Screams of those injured or trapped were barely audible at first, as our minds struggled to grapple with the reality before us: a massive, four-story building reduced to pile of rubble; dust, mixing with smoke and fire, obscuring the view of the little that was left.

Because we had thought that the sound of the explosion was still related to a single rocket or shell, most of the marines had run toward the foxholes and bunkers, while we—the chaplains—had gone to the scene of the noise, "just in case" someone had been wounded. Now, as news spread quickly throughout the camp—news of the magnitude of the tragedy; news of the need for others to run to the aid of those comrades who might still be alive—marines came from all directions.

There was a sense of God's presence that day in the small miracles of life which we encountered in each body that, despite all odds, still had a breath within. But there was more of His presence, more to keep our faith alive, in the heroism—and in the *humanity*—of the men who responded to the cries for help.

We saw marines risk their own lives again and again, as they went into the smoke and the fire to try to pull someone out, or as they worked to uncover friends, all the while knowing that further collapse of huge pieces of concrete, precariously perched like dominoes, could easily crush the rescuers.

There was humanity at its best that day, and a reminder not to give up the hope and dreams of what the world *could be*, in the tears that could still be shed by these men, regardless of how cynical they had pretended to be before; regardless of how much they might have seen before.

Certain images will stay with me, always. Sometimes we read of looting during tragedies. That day I remember a marine who found a wad of money amidst the rubble. He held it at arm's length as if it were dirty and cried out for a match or a lighter so that it could be burned. No one that day wanted to profit from the suffering of the catastrophe. Later, the chaplains would put the word out that the money should be collected and given to us, for we were sure that a fund for widows and orphans would ultimately be established. But, at that moment, I was hypnotized with the rest of the men and watched as the money was burned.

Working with the wounded—sometimes comforting, and simply letting them know help was on the way; sometimes trying to pull and carry those whose injuries appeared less dangerous in an immediate sense than the approaching fire or the smothering smoke—my *kippa* was lost. The last I remember it, I has used it to mop someone's brow. Father Pucciarelli, the Catholic chaplain, cut a circle out of his cap, a piece of camouflage cloth that would become my temporary head-covering. Somehow, we wanted those marines to know not just that we were chaplains, but that he was Christian and that I was Jewish. Somehow, we both wanted to shout the message in a land where people were killing each other, at least partially based on the differences in religion among them, that *we*—we Americans—still believed that we could be proud of our particular religions and yet work side by side when the time came to help others, to comfort, and to ease pain.

Father Pucciarelli and I worked that day as brothers. The words from the prophet Malachi kept recurring to me, words he had uttered some twenty-five hundred years ago as he had looked around at fighting and cruelty and pain: "Have we not all one Father?" he asked. "Has not one God created us all?" It was painfully obvious, tragically obvious, that our world still could not show that we had learned to answer "yes." Still, I thought, perhaps some of us *can keep the question alive*. Some of us can cry out—as the marines did that day—that we believe the answer is yes.

Before the bombing, Pooch and I had been in a building perhaps a hundred yards away. There had been one other chaplain, Lieutenant Danny Wheeler, a Protestant minister, who had spent the night in the building that was attacked. Pooch and I were so sure that he was dead that we had promised each other that, when the day came to return to the States, we would visit his wife together. Suddenly, Pooch noticed Danny's stole—what we used to call his Protestant tallit. Because it was far from the area Danny was supposed to have been in, there was cautious hope that perhaps he had been thrown clear, that perhaps he had survived.

Later, Danny would tell the story of his terror. He was under the rubble, alive, not knowing what had happened, and not knowing how badly he was hurt. The first voices he had heard upon awakening were Lebanese—voices of volunteers who had come to help our troops during the rescue attempt. For him, however, their voices were frightening: perhaps these were enemy troops who had overrun our camp.

He was afraid to cry out, he later told us. If these were enemy soldiers, perhaps they would shoot him. Then—and this statement of his gives me an inkling of the terror that filled him—he began to think that perhaps being shot was preferable to any other alternative at that time: preferably to dying slowly in such terrifying isolation.

Before he had to make a choice, American voices came through. These were the voices of the marines searching near his stole, and his cry for help at that time was answered with digging which lasted four hours before he was dragged out alive.

Danny told me later that I treated him like a newborn baby when he came out: that I counted fingers and toes, trying to see that he was whole. I didn't realize that I was so obvious, but the truth us that we could not believe that he was in one piece.

As I hugged him as they brought over a stretcher, he spoke, and I can still hear his first words. Racked with pain, still unsure of his own condition, he asked how his clerk was. Like so many of the men we would save that day, he asked first about the others. These men, the survivors, still had no idea of the extent of the damage; they still thought that perhaps they had been in the one area of the building hit by rocket or mortar. We would wait until later to sit with these men and tell them the truth, to share with them the magnitude of the tragedy.

After the living were taken out, there was much more work to be done. With the wounded, with those who had survived, there was the strange job of trying to ease a gnawing feeling of guilt that would slowly surface: guilt that they had somehow let down their comrades by not dying with them. So, our job was to tell them how every life saved was important to us: how their survival was important to our faith, and our hope. They had to give thanks—with us—that they still had the gift, and the responsibility, of lives that would go on.

With others, the marines who stayed behind to continue the job of digging—a terrible, horrifying job of collecting human parts for iden-tification and for eventual burial—there was the job of comforting them as they mourned. Thankfully, the self-defense mechanisms within us took over from time to time, and we were able to work without reacting to each and every horror we would encounter. But, suddenly, something would trigger our emotions; something would touch our humanity in a way impossible to avoid.

For some, it would be the finding of a friend's body, someone filled with life only days before. For others, it would be a scrap of paper or a simple belonging—a birthday card, or a picture of someone's children—which would remind them that this was no abstract "body count" of two hundred and forty military casualties. This was a tragedy of *people*, where each was unique, and each had a story. Each had a past, and each had been cheated of a future. As the Mishnah puts it, each was a world. We were not digging up "two hundred and forty." We were digging up one, plus one, plus one . . .

I have a personal memory of two "things" that brought to my mind images of life, images that haunt me still. One was a packet of three envelopes, tied together with a rubber band. On top, under the band, was a note that read, "To be mailed in case of death." The other was a Red Cross message, delivered the next morning. The American Red Cross is the agency used by navy families to communicate medical news from home. This message was a birth announcement: a baby had been born, and we were to deliver the good news. Only now there was no father we could congratulate, no father to whom the news could be conveyed.

That message stayed on the chaplain's desk for days. Somehow, we couldn't throw it away. And yet we didn't know what to do with it. So it stayed on the desk. And, without mentioning it, we all seemed to avoid that desk. . . .

I stayed in Beirut for four more days before finally returning to Italy and to my family. During those days, as the work went on, a marine here or there would send a silent signal that he wanted me—that is, *a chaplain*—near. Sometimes it was to talk. Sometimes it was so that he could shrug his shoulders or lift his eyes in despair. Sometimes it was just to feel that I was near—for, despite the struggles I might be feeling on a personal level, I was a *chaplain*, and therefore a symbol that there was room for hope, and for dreams, even at the worst of times.

In Jewish tradition, of course, when we visit the home of a mourner during *shiva*, the first week following the death of a loved one, visitors follow a simple rule. If a mourner initiates the conversation, the visitor responds. Otherwise, you sit in silence, communicating concern through your very presence, even without words. Somehow, I applied the rules of shiva during these days of digging. When a soldier or sailor said something, I responded; otherwise, I stood by.

During all of my visits to Beirut, I, along with other chaplains, spent much time simply speaking with the men. Informal discussions, whether going on while crouched in a foxhole or strolling toward the tent set up for chow, were just as important as anything formal we might set up. I remember the first time I jumped in a foxhole, the first time the shells actually fell within the U.S. area. Looking around at the others in there with me, I made the remark that we probably had set up the only "interfaith foxholes" in Beirut! The Druze, Muslims, Christians, all had theirs. The Jewish forces in the Israeli Army had theirs. But we were together. I made the comment then that perhaps if the world had more interfaith foxholes, there might be less of a need for foxholes altogether.

To understand the role of the chaplain—Jewish, Catholic, or Protestant—is to understand that we try to remind others, and perhaps ourselves as well, to cling to our humanity, even in the worst of times. We bring with us the wisdom of men and women whose faith has kept alive their dreams in ages past. We bring with us the images of what the world *could be*, of what we ourselves *might be*, drawn from the visions of prophets and the promises of our holy books. We bring with us the truth that faith not only reminds us of the Holy in Heaven, but also of the holiness we can create here on earth. It brings not only a message of what is divine, but also of what it means to be truly human.

It is too easy to give in to despair in a world sometimes seemingly filled with cruelty and brutality. But we must remember not just the depths to which humans might sink, but also the heights to which they may aspire.

That October day in Beirut saw men reach heroic heights, indeed: heights of physical endurance and courage, to be sure; but heights of sacrifice, compassion, kindness, and simple human decency as well. And—even if the admission might bring a blush to the cheeks of a few of the marines—heights of love.

Long ago, the rabbis offered one interpretation of the Biblical verse that tells us that we are created "in the image of God." It does not refer to physical likeness, they explained, but to spiritual potential. We have within us the power to reflect as God's creatures the highest values of our Creator. As God is forgiving and merciful, so can we be. As He is caring and kind, so must we strive to be. As He is filled with love, so must we be.

Because of the actions I witnessed during that hell in Beirut, I glimpsed at least a fleeting image of heaven. For, in the hearts and hands of men who chose to act as brothers, I glimpsed God's hand as well. I did not stand alone to face a world forsaken by God; I felt I was part of one created with infinite care, and wonderful—awesome— potential.

We live in a world where it is not hard to find cause for despair. The chaplain has the challenge to bring to those who often see terror at its worst some reason for hope.

We need to keep faith and to keep searching, even during the worst of times. Only then may we find strength enough to keep believing that the best of times still might be.

Notes

ABBREVIATIONS

AJA-CC = American Jewish Archives–Chaplaincy Collection
AJHS-JWBC = American Jewish Historical Society–Jewish Welfare Board
   Collection
NA-AGO-JS = National Archives–Adjutant General's Office–Jewish Section
NA-CCC-RG 247 = National Archives–Chief of Chaplains Collection–Record Group 247
NYPL-JD = New York Public Library–Jewish Division
RACHD Museum = Royal Army Chaplains' Department Museum
VC-USACS = Voorsanger Collection–U.S. Army Chaplain Museum and
   School

NOTES TO CHAPTER 1

1. The Torah, Exodus 17:8–13.
2. Ibid., Deuteronomy 20:2–4.
3. Drury, *History,* Vol. 1, 2.
4. Smith, *The Military Ordinariate,* 12.
5. Smith, *The Navy and Its Chaplains,* 5.
6. Ibid., 19.
7. Thompson, *Army Chaplaincy,* Introduction.
8. Honeywell, *Chaplaincy,* 11.
9. Ibid., 23.
10. Brinsfield, "Our Roots for Ministry," *Military Chaplains Review* (Fall 1987): 26–27.
11. Ibid., 29. Department of the Army, "A Brief History," U.S. Army Center of Military History, 3.
12. Smith, *The Military Ordinariate,* 61.

13. Norton, *Struggling for Recognition,* 27.
14. Drury, *History,* Vol. 1, 62.
15. Prucha, *Broadax and Bayonet,* 210.
16. Norton, *Struggling for Recognition,* 71; Drury, *History,* Vol. 1, 117.
17. Drazin and Currey, *For God and Country,* 25.
18. Ibid., 26.
19. Karp, *Haven and Home,* 7.
20. Sachar, *Modern Jewish History,* 179.
21. Brinsfield, "Our Roots for Ministry," *Military Chaplains Review* (Fall 1987): 30.
22. Blau and Baron, *The Jews of the United States,* 33.
23. Sachar, *Modern Jewish History,* 183.
24. Ibid., 193.

NOTES TO CHAPTER 2

1. Shattuck, *A Shield,* 11.
2. Norton, *Struggling for Recognition,* 124.
3. Shattuck, *A Shield,* 57.
4. Korn, "Jewish Chaplains," *American Jewish Archives* 1:7.
5. Winey, "Clergy In Uniform," *Military Images* 4 (June 1983).
6. Hammond, *Army Chaplain's Manual,* 72.
7. Young, *Where They Lie,* 15.
8. Korn, "Jewish Chaplains," *American Jewish Archives* 1:8.
9. Ibid., 9.
10. Korn, *American Jewry,* 58.
11. *Encyclopedia Judaica,* 1149.
12. Korn, *American Jewry,* 63.
13. Ibid., 64.
14. Ibid.
15. Ibid., 65.
16. Ibid., 66.
17. "Petitions to the United States Senate," AJA-CC.
18. Korn, *American Jewry,* 70.
19. Ibid., 71.
20. Brown, *The Army Chaplain,* 23.
21. Korn, *American Jewry,* 83.
22. "Monthly Reports of Chaplain Gotthelf to Surgeon General," AJA-CC.

23. Korn, "Jewish Chaplains," *American Jewish Archives* 1:20.

24. "1900 Annual Report of the Adjutant General of the State of New York," U.S. Army Military History Institute, 820.

25. "Rabbi Max del Banco Material," AJA-CC.

26. Korn, *American Jewry*, 89.

27. Byrne and Soman, eds., *Your True Marcus*, 163.

28. "Correspondence between Dr. Jacob R. Marcus and Dr. Louis Ginsberg," AJA-CC.

29. "Chaplain A. D. Cohen Letter of Resignation," National Archives–Rebel Archives.

30. Smith, *The Military Ordinariate*, 71.

31. Ibid., 72.

32. Redkey, "Black Chaplains in the Union Army," *Civil War History* 33 (December 1987): 331–35.

33. Norton, *Struggling for Recognition*, 86.

34. The first female chaplains came into the services in the 1970s.

35. McPherson, *Battle Cry of Freedom*, 620.

36. Ibid., 622.

37. Ibid.

38. Korn, *American Jewry*, 162.

39. Ibid., 178.

40. Ibid., 186.

41. Higham, *Strangers in the Land*, 13.

42. Cohen, *Encounter with Emancipation*, 149.

NOTES TO CHAPTER 3

1. Belth, *A Promise to Keep*, 25.

2. Ibid.

3. Higham, *Strangers in the Land*, 62.

4. Cohen, *Encounter with Emancipation*, 250–51.

5. Ahlstrom, *A Religious History*, 854.

6. Cohen, *Encounter with Emancipation*, 250–51.

7. Wolf, *The American Jew*, 1.

8. Mosesson, *The Jewish War Veterans Story*, 17.

9. Cohen, *Encounter with Emancipation*, 279.

10. Ibid., 279.

11. Ibid., 283.

12. Kohler, ed., *Selected Addresses and Papers of Simon Wolf*, 19.

13. Ibid., 197.

14. Adler, ed., *American Jewish Yearbook*, 1900.

15. Mosesson, *The Jewish War Veterans Story*, 19.

16. "Letter to Army Adjutant General Regarding Jewish High Holidays," NA-AGO-JS.

17. "Letter to Mr. Simon Wolf of the Union of American Hebrew Congregations," NA-AGO-JS.

18. "Letter to Rabbi Dr. H. Pereira Mendes from Elihu Root," NA-AGO-JS.

19. "Letter from *Jewish Daily News* to Honorable Elihu Root," NA-AGO-JS.

20. "Letter from Elihu Root to Congressman William Sulzer," NA-AGO-JS.

21. "Memorandum from War Department to Congressman Henry Goldfogle," NA-AGO-JS.

22. "Preamble to Resolutions Adopted at Meeting Federation of Jewish Organizations, State of New York," December 29, 1908, NYPL-JD.

23. Ibid.

24. Ibid.

25. "Address given by Congressman William Sulzer to meeting of Federation of Jewish Organizations, State of New York," NYPL-JD.

26. Ibid.

27. *American Israelite*, October 8, 1908, 1.

28. Ibid., February 10, 1910.

29. *Hebrew Standard*, June 15, 1911, 2.

30. "Letter from War Department to Mr. Nissim Behar," NA-AGO-JS.

31. "Announcement of Founding of Patriotic League of America," NYPL-JD.

32. Ibid.

33. Ibid.

34. "A Bill to Increase the Number of Chaplains in the Army," Sixty-second Congress, April 25, 1912, U.S. Army Military History Institute, 7.

35. Ibid.

36. Ibid.

37. *American Israelite*, November 5, 1914, 5.

38. *Chicago Sentinel*, October 5, 1916, 11.

39. "Memorandum from Adjutant General of the Army to Major LeRoy Eltingle," NA-AGO-JS.

40. "Memorandum to Congressman Chandler from Secretary of War Lindley M. Garrison," NA-AGO-JS.
41. Belth, *A Promise to Keep,* 64.
42. "Messages from Commanding Officers Concerning Jewish Holidays," NA-AGO-JS.
43. "Jews in the United States Army and Navy," Adler, ed., *American Jewish Yearbook,* 1916, 1–4.
44. Sachar, *Modern Jewish History,* 81–82.
45. Ibid.
46. Interview with Mrs. Bertha Feldman, February 1990.
47. "Letter from Rabbi Shapo to Dr. Rosenau," AJA-CC.
48. "Letter from Synagog Extension to Rabbi Landman," AJA-CC.
49. "Letter from Dr. Rosenau to Rabbi Landman," AJA-CC.
50. "Report from Rabbi Landman about His Activities," AJA-CC.
51. "Rabbi Landman's Account of Holiday Services," AJA-CC.

NOTES TO CHAPTER 4

1. Link, *American Epoch,* 198.
2. Higham, *Strangers in the Land,* 216.
3. "Annual Report," 1919, AJHS-JWBC.
4. Ibid.
5. Goren, *New York Jews,* Chapter 10.
6. Janowsky, Kraft, and Postal, *Change and Challenge,* 7.
7. "Annual Report," 1919, AJHS-JWBC.
8. *Encyclopedia Judaica,* 274.
9. "Annual Report," 1919, AJHS-JWBC.
10. Ahlstrom, *A Religious History,* 889.
11. Sheerin, *Never Look Back,* 44–45.
12. Ibid.
13. "Rabbi Jacob Singer Correspondence File," AJA-CC.
14. "Jewish Welfare Board," 1917, AJHS-JWBC.
15. "Annual Report," 1919, AJHS-JWBC.
16. Janowsky, Kraft, and Postal, *Change and Challenge,* 8.
17. "Annual Report," 1919, AJHS-JWBC.
18. "Jewish Welfare Board," 1918, AJHS-JWBC.
19. "Annual Report," 1919, AJHS-JWBC.
20. Smith, *The Military Ordinariate,* 104.
21. *American Hebrew,* September 14, 1917, 523.

22. "Annual Report," 1919, AJHS-JWBC.
23. *American Hebrew*, October 12, 1917, 638.
24. Smith, *The Military Ordinariate*, 112.
25. Nave, *Nave's Handbook*, 47.
26. *Menorah Journal*, October–December 1919.
27. "Letter from Rabbi Voorsanger to His Parents," May 14, 1917, VC-USACS.
28. "Letter from Rabbi Voorsanger to a San Francisco Newspaper," April 1918, VC-USACS.
29. *New York Times*, October 12, 1919, 8.
30. "Correspondence of Rabbi Benjamin Friedman," AJA-CC.
31. Barish, ed., *Rabbis*, 10.
32. Ibid.
33. *New York Times*, October 12, 1919, 8.
34. Levinger, *A Jewish Chaplain in France*, 8.
35. Ibid., 51.
36. "Experiences of a Jewish Chaplain on the Western Front," pamphlet circa 1920, RACHD Museum, 33–57.
37. *Bilder und Texte aus der Soldatenseelsorge, 1550–1945.*
38. "Rabbi Jacob Sonderling Correspondence," AJA-CC.
39. *Bilder und Texte aus der Soldatenseelsorge, 1550–1945.*
40. "Army Correspondence Concerning Jewish Insignia," NA-CCC-RG 247.
41. Ibid.
42. Ibid.
43. *Army and Navy Journal*, July 20, 1918, 1788.
44. "Rabbi David Goldberg Correspondence," AJA-CC.
45. Ibid.
46. Goldberg, *Sky Piloting the Great Lakes*, 51.

NOTES TO CHAPTER 5

1. Weigley, *History of the United States Army*, 396.
2. Drury, *History*, Vol. 1, 204–5.
3. "First Report on War Emergency Activities," July 1919, AJHS-JWBC, 67.
4. Janowsky, Kraft, and Postal, *Change and Challenge*, 17.
5. "The JWB First Report on War Emergency Activities," 1920, AJHS-JWBC, 82.

6. Ibid., 85.

7. Ibid., 86.

8. Ibid., 87.

9. "Report of the Army and Navy Committee," October 31, 1922, AJHS-JWBC, 43.

10. Cohen, *Encounter with Emancipation,* 245.

11. Ribuffo, "Henry Ford and the International Jews," *American Jewish History* 4 (June 1980): 452–57.

12. Link, *American Epoch,* 341.

13. "Jews on University Facilities," *Contemporary Jewish Record* (May–June 1939): 87.

14. "Letter from the Secretary of the Academic Board for the Superintendent of the United States Naval Academy," Special Collections–Nimitz Library, United States Naval Academy.

15. Belth, *A Promise to Keep,* 112.

16. Lasker, "Jewish Handicaps in the Employment Market," *Jewish Social Service Quarterly* 3 (March 1926): 170–74.

17. "Report of the Subcommittees of the Senate and House Committees on Military Affairs," April 16, 1924, U.S. Army Military History Institute, 34.

18. Ibid., 37.

19. U.S. War Department, *The Chaplain,* 13.

20. Ibid., 14.

21. Gushwa, *The Best and Worst of Times,* 40.

22. "1936 Annual Report, Army and Navy Committee," AJHS-JWBC, 2.

23. Kraut, "Towards the Establishment of the National Conference of Christians and Jews," *American Jewish History* 3 (March 1988): 400.

24. Waldman, "The International Scene in Jewish Life," 19.

25. Belth, "Problems of Anti-Semitism," 50–51.

26. Brinkley, *Voices of Protest,* 266.

27. Athans, "The Fahey-Coughlin Connection."

28. *Sentinel,* 8 June 1939, 1.

29. "1937 Annual Report, Army and Navy Committee," AJHS-JWBC, 2.

30. Janowsky, Kraft, and Postal, *Change and Challenge,* 33.

NOTES TO CHAPTER 6

1. "Bureau of War Report," December 1944, AJHS-JWBC, 2.

2. Weigley, *History of the United States Army,* 427.

3. Ibid., 435.

4. Honeywell, *Chaplains,* 215.

5. Ibid., 208.

6. Drury, *History,* Vol. 2, 51.

7. Honeywell, *Chaplains,* 248.

8. Drury, *History,* Vol. 2, 62.

9. Ibid., 24.

10. "Report of the Army and Navy Committee," March 1941, AJHS-JWBC.

11. "Annual Jewish Welfare Board Report 1941," December 1941, AJHS-JWBC, 3–4.

12. "Letter from Aryeh Lev to Louis Kraft," March 19, 1941, AJHS-JWBC.

13. Hoenig, *The Orthodox Rabbi as a Military Chaplain,* 35–60.

14. Interview with Rabbi Joshua Goldberg, November 1990.

15. "Public Relations Committee Organizational Outline," July 1941, AJHS-JWBC.

16. "Copy of Chaplain Aryeh Lev's Speech," March 1, 1941, AJHS-JWBC.

17. "Letter from Rabbi James G. Heller," August 20, 1941, AJHS-JWBC.

18. Smith, *The Military Ordinariate,* 155.

19. Bernstein, *Rabbis at War,* 18–22.

20. Brickner, "What's What with Chaplaincies," *Hebrew Union College Monthly* (March 1942): 314–16.

21. Bernstein, *Rabbis at War,* 8.

22. "Memorandum of Conference of Jewish Chaplains," February 1942, AJHS-JWBC.

23. Wyman, *The Abandonment of the Jews,* 9.

24. Interview with Rabbi Eric Friedland, November 1986.

25. National Conference of Christians and Jews pamphlet, NA-CCC-RG 247.

26. "1942 Annual JWB Report," AJHS-JWBC.

27. "Memorandum from Aryeh Lev to the JWB," December 1942, AJHS-JWBC.

28. "Four Chaplains Collection," United States Army Center of Military History.

29. Ibid.

30. Barish, ed., *Rabbis,* 321.

31. Ibid., 307.

32. Ibid., 310.

33. Gushwa, *The Best and Worst of Times,* 114–15.

34. Interview with Rabbi Joshua Goldberg, November 1990.

35. "1943 Navy Chaplain's Report," March 1943, AJHS-JWBC.

36. Ibid.

37. "A Report of the Jewish Chaplain's Conference," July 1943, AJHS-JWBC.

38. Ibid.

39. Barish, ed., *Rabbis,* 157–58.

40. Army Chief of Chaplains, "The Chaplain Serves: 1943 Annual Report," March 1944, AJHS-JWBC.

41. Frank and Shaw, *Victory and Occupation,* 727.

42. "Papers Related to Case of New Testament Controversy," May 1943, AJHS-JWBC.

43. Ibid.

44. "Rabbi Bennett Correspondence with JWB," August 1943, AJHS-JWBC.

45. Interview with Rabbi Joshua Goldberg, November 1990.

46. Zehavy, ed., *Chaplain on Wings,* 11.

47. Jewish Welfare Board, *Responsa in War Time,* Introduction, AJHS-JWBC.

48. Ibid., 59.

49. Ibid., 60.

50. Ibid.

51. Smith, *The Military Ordinariate,* 171.

52. "Memorandum for the Adjutant General of the Army from Brigadier General William A. Arnold," May 1944, NA-CCC-RG 247.

53. "Bureau of War Records–Annual Report," December 1944, AJHS-JWBC.

54. Interview with Rabbi Herschel Schacter, February 1992.

55. "Letter from Chaplain Bryant to Chaplain Arnold," May 1945, NA-CCC-RG 247.

56. Gittelsohn, *Here I Am—Harnessed to Hope,* Chapter 9.

57. Interview with Rabbi Roland Gittelsohn, May 1992.

58. Barish, ed., *Rabbis,* 305.

59. Grobman, *Rekindling,* 9.

60. "CANRA Report on Displaced Persons," March 1946, AJHS-JWBC.

61. Grobman, *Rekindling,* 49.

62. Ibid., 50.

63. Ibid., 7.

64. Ibid., 56.

65. Interview with Rabbi Abraham Klausner, February 1998.

66. Ibid.
67. Ibid.
68. "Letter from Rabbi Klausner to CANRA," AJHS-JWBC.
69. Grobman, *Rekindling*, 72.
70. Interview with Rabbi Abraham Klausner, February 1998.
71. Grobman, *Rekindling*, 74.
72. Nadich, *Eisenhower and the Jews*, Chapter 3.
73. Lipson, "Patton's DP Camps," *Moment* (February 1997): 96.
74. Grobman, *Rekindling*, 130.

NOTES TO CHAPTER 7

1. Weigley, *History of the United States Army*, 519.
2. Drury, *History*, Vol. 6, 168.
3. Janowsky, Kraft, and Postal, *Change and Challenge*, 55.
4. Ibid.
5. Drury, *History*, Vol. 6, 173.
6. Chaplain Sam Sobel, Chaplain Resource Board–Oral History, Norfolk, Va.
7. Barish, ed., *Rabbis*, 149.
8. Ibid., 142.
9. Venzke, *Confidence in Battle*, 138.
10. Ibid., 139.
11. Bergsma, *Chaplains with Marines in Vietnam*, 70.
12. Ibid., 150–51.
13. Ackermann, *He Was Always There*, 26.
14. "Undated newspaper article—Rabbi E. David Lapp," circa December 1966, JWB–Jewish Chaplains Council Archives.
15. *Boston Globe*, April 13, 1967, 14.
16. "Undated newspaper article–Lt. Harold Vogel," circa April 1967, JWB–Jewish Chaplains Council Archives.
17. Winograd, *The Jungle Jews of Vietnam*, 25.
18. Ibid., 87.
19. Currey and Drazin, *For God and Country*, 1.
20. Ibid., 2.
21. Ibid., 197–99.
22. Rabbi Arnold Resnicoff, Appendix in this volume.
23. "Undated JWB Pamphlet Regarding Commission on Jewish Chaplaincy Activities," JWB–Jewish Chaplains Council Archives.

24. Bletter and Grinker, *The Invisible Thread,* 147.

25. *New York Times,* March 26, 1986, 1.

26. Interview with Rabbi Norman Auerback, April 1989.

27. "Correspondence between Chaplain Romer and JWB," March 1991, JWB–Jewish Chaplains Council.

28. "Public Affairs Release from the USS *Saratoga,*" November 1990, JWB–Jewish Chaplains Council.

29. "Report of Captain Bill Peterson to JWB," March 21, 1991, JWB–Jewish Chaplains Council.

30. Ibid.

31. Ibid.

32. "Transcript of telephone conversation between Chaplain Zalis and JWB," January, 20, 1991, JWB–Jewish Chaplains Council.

33. "Written account of Passover Programs from Rabbi Zalis," April 3, 1991, JWB–Jewish Chaplains Council.

34. Ibid.

35. Ibid.

36. *Jewish Exponent,* April 19, 1991, 25–26.

37. *Jewish Week,* May 3, 1991, 35–36.

38. Unpublished article by Chaplain Mitchell Schranz.

39. Chaplain Pierce, a devout Christian, would work for weeks to help ensure that visiting rabbis would have maximum attendance at seder meals.

Bibliography

PRIMARY SOURCES — MAJOR COLLECTIONS AND
ARCHIVAL DATA

American Jewish Archives–Jacob Rader Marcus Center, Chaplaincy Collection, Cincinnati, Ohio.

American Jewish Historical Society, Aryeh Lev Papers and Jewish Welfare Board Archives, Waltham, Massachusetts.

Department of the Army, U.S. Army Chaplain Museum and School, Chaplaincy Archives and Elkan Voorsanger Collection, Fort Jackson, South Carolina.

Department of the Navy, Chaplain Resource Board, Norfolk, Virginia.

National Archives, Chief of Chaplains Collection, Correspondence of the Army Adjutant General's Office–Jewish Section, Washington, D.C.

New York Public Library, Jewish Division, New York City.

U.S. Army Center of Military History, Chaplaincy Collection, Washington, D.C.

U.S. Army Military History Institute, Chaplaincy Collection, Carlisle Barracks, Pennsylvania.

U.S. Naval Academy, Academy Archives, Annapolis, Maryland.

NEWSPAPERS

American Hebrew, September 14, 1917, 523; October 12, 1917, 638; October 18, 1918, 616.

American Israelite, October 8, 1908, 1; November 5, 1914, 5; July 20, 1916; August 6, 1916.

Army and Navy Journal, June 29, 1918, 1672; July 20, 1918, 1788.

Boston Globe, April 13, 1967, 14.

Chicago Sentinel, October 5, 1916, 11.

Hebrew Standard, June 15, 1911, 2.

Jewish Exponent, April 19, 1991, 25–26.

Jewish Telegraphic Association, September 29, 1987.

Jewish Week, May 3, 1991, 35–36.

New York Times, October 12, 1919, 8; March 26, 1986, 1; April 19, 1991.

Sentinel, June 8, 1939, 1.

PERSONAL INTERVIEWS

Feldman, Bertha, January 21, 1990, North Miami Beach, Florida.

Freehof, Rabbi Solomon, April 1, 1990, by phone .

Friedland, Rabbi Eric, chaplain, October 12, 1986, Chicago, Illinois.

Gittelsohn, Rabbi Roland, chaplain, May 18, 1993, by phone.

Goldberg, Rabbi Joshua, chaplain, November 22, 1992, West Palm Beach, Florida.

Klausner, Rabbi Abraham, chaplain, February, 9, 1998, by phone.

Lorge, Rabbi Ernest, chaplain, November 14, 1986, by phone.

Schacter, Rabbi Herschel, chaplain, February 24, 1992, New York City.

ARTICLES

Belth, Nathan C. "Problems of Anti-Semitism." *Contemporary Jewish Record* (July–August 1939): 43–55.

Brickner, Barnett, R. "What's What with Chaplaincies." *Hebrew Union College Monthly* (March 1942): 314–16.

Brinsfield, John W. "Our Roots for Ministry: The Continental Army, General Washington and the Free Exercise of Religion." *Military Chaplains Review* (Fall 1987): 23–33.

Doughtery, Kevin. "The Impact of Religion on General Stonewall Jackson." *Military Chaplains Review* (Spring 1990): 61–65.

Feinstein, Martin. "Verse From the Trenches." *Menorah Journal* (December 1916): 337–39.

Greenberg, Mark I. "Ambivalent Relations: Acceptance and Anti-Semitism in Confederate Thomasville." *American Jewish Archives* 45 (Summer 1993): 13–25.

Hoenig, Sidney B. *The Orthodox Rabbi as a Military Chaplain.* Rabbinical Council of America, 1976.

Hourihan, William J. "Chaplain Alfred A. Pruden and the Professionalization of the U.S. Army, 1899–1920." *Military Chaplains Review* (November 1988): 11–17.

"Jewish Communal Life in the United States." *Jewish Social Service Quarterly* 3 (November 1924): 18–21.

"Jews on University Faculties." *Contemporary Jewish Record* (May–June 1939): 86–87.

Konowitz, Mordecai. "The Jew in the Army." *Menorah Journal* (June 1918): 154–61.

Korn, Bertram W. "Jewish Chaplains in the Civil War." *American Jewish Archives* 1 (1948): 6–23.

Kraut, Benny. "Towards the Establishment of the National Conference of Christians and Jews." *American Jewish History* 3 (March 1988): 400.

Lasker, Bruno. "Jewish Handicaps in the Employment Market." *Jewish Social Service Quarterly* 3 (March 1926): 170–74.

Lehman, Irving. "Our Duty as Americans." *Menorah Journal* (February 1918): 6–10.

Lipson, Alfred. "Patton's DP Camps." *Moment* (February 1997): 52–98.

Miller, Joel L. "The A. E. F. Menorah in France." *Menorah Journal* (October–December 1919): 299–302.

Quimby, Rollin W. "The Chaplain's Predicament." *Civil War History* 8 (March 1962): 25–37.

Redkey, Edwin S. "Black Chaplains in the Union Army." *Civil War History* 33 (December 1987): 331–49.

Ribuffo, Leo P. "Henry Ford and the International Jews." *American Jewish History* 4 (June 1980): 452–57.

Stearns, Harold E. "A Gentile's Picture of the Jew." *Menorah Journal* 2 (December 1916): 273–79.

Steele, Richard W. "The War on Intolerance: The Reformation of American Nationalism, 1939–1941." *Journal of American Ethnic History* (Fall 1989): 14.

Waldman, Morris D. "The International Scene in Jewish Life." *Jewish Social Service Quarterly* (December 1932): 19–25.

Winey, Michael J. "Clergy In Uniform." *Military Images* 4 (June 1983): 8–12.

BOOKS

Ackermann, Henry F. *He Was Always There: The U.S. Army Ministry in Vietnam.* Washington, D.C.: Army Chief of Chaplains, 1989.

Adler, Cyrus, ed. *The American Jewish Yearbook.* New York: American Jewish Committee, 1900, 1916, 1918, 1919.

Ahlstrom, Sydney E. *A Religious History of the American People.* New Haven: Yale University Press, 1972.

Athans, Mary. "The Fahey-Coughlin Connection." Ann Arbor: University Microfilms, 1982.

Barish, Louis, ed. *Rabbis in Uniform.* New York: Jonathan David Publishers, 1962.

Bayor, Ronald H. *Neighbors in Conflict.* Baltimore: Johns Hopkins University Press, 1978.

Belth, Nathan C. *A Promise to Keep: A Narrative of the American Encounter with Anti-Semitism.* New York: Schocken Books, 1981.

Bergsma, Herbert L. *Chaplains with Marines in Vietnam, 1962–1971.* Washington, D.C.: U.S. Marine Corps, 1985.

Berkowitz, Henry J. *Boot Camp.* Philadelphia: Jewish Publication Society of America, 1948.

Bernstein, Philip S. *Rabbis at War.* Waltham, MA: American Jewish Historical Society, 1971.

Bilder und Texte aus der Soldatenseelsorge, 1550–1945 [Pictures and Text of the German Army Chaplains Newspaper]. Bonn: Herausgegeben vom Evangelischen Kirchenamt für die Bundeswehr, 1983.

Blau, Joseph L., and Salo W. Baron. *The Jews of the United States: A Documentary History, 1790–1840.* New York: Columbia University Press, 1963.

Bletter, Diana, and Lori Grinker, *The Invisible Thread: A Portrait of Jewish American Women.* Philadelphia: Jewish Publication Society, 1989.

Brinkley, Alan. *Voices of Protest.* New York: Alfred A. Knopf, 1982.

Brown, W. Y. *The Army Chaplain.* Philadelphia: William S. and Alfred Martien, 1863.

Butler, Jon. *Awash in a Sea of Faith.* Cambridge: 1990.

Byrne, Frank and Jean Powers Soman, eds. *Your True Marcus.* Kent, Ohio: Kent State University Press, 1985.

Cohen, Naomi. *Encounter with Emancipation.* Philadelphia: Jewish Publication Society of America, 1984.

———. *Not Free to Desist: The American Jewish Committee.* Philadelphia: Jewish Publication Society of America, 1972.

Commission on Jewish Chaplaincy, National Jewish Welfare Board. *Responsa in War Time.* New York: Jewish Welfare Board, 1947.

Cox, Harvey G., ed. *Military Chaplains: From a Religious Military to a Military Religion.* New York: American Report Press, 1971.

Crosby, Donald. *Battlefield Chaplains: Catholic Priests in World War II.* Laurence: University Press of Kansas, 1994.

Dempsey, Martin, ed. *The Priest Among the Soldiers.* London: Publisher unknown, 1947.

Drazin, Israel, and Cecil B. Currey. *For God and Country.* Hoboken, N.J.: Ktav Publishing Company, 1995.

Drury, Clifford M. *The History of the Chaplain Corps, United States Navy.* Volumes 1, 2, and 6. Washington, D.C.: Department of the Navy, 1983.

————. *United States Naval Chaplains: Biographical and Service Record Sketches.* Washington, D.C.: Department of the Navy, 1957.

Elkins, Dov Peretz. *God's Warriors.* New York: Jonathan David, 1974.

Eltingle, LeRoy. *The Psychology of War.* Leavenworth: Army Service School, 1915.

Encyclopedia Judaica, Jerusalem: Keter Publishing Company, 1971.

Finkelstein, Louis, ed. *The Jews: Their History, Culture and Religion.* Philadelphia: Jewish Publication Society of America, 1960.

Frank, Benis M., and Henry I. Shaw. *Victory and Occupation.* Washington, D.C.: Headquarters, United States Marine Corps, 1968.

Gerber, David, ed. *Anti-Semitism in American History.* Chicago: University of Illinois Press, 1986.

Germain, Dom Aidan H. *Catholic Military and Naval Chaplains.* Washington, D.C.: University of America, 1929.

Gittelsohn, Roland B. *Here Am I—Harnessed to Hope.* New York: Vantage Press, 1985.

Goldberg, David. *Sky Piloting the Great Lakes.* Great Lakes, Corps of Chaplains, U.S. Navy, 1920.

Gordon, Harold H. *Chaplains on Wings.* New York: Shengold Publishers, 1981.

Goren, Arthur A. *New York Jews and the Quest for Community.* New York: Columbia University Press, 1970.

Grobman, Alex. *Rekindling the Flame.* Detroit: Wayne State University Press, 1993.

Gumpertz, Sydney G. *The Jewish Legion of Valor.* New York: Sydney G. Gumpertz Publisher, 1934.

Gushwa, Robert L. *The Best and Worst of Times: The United States Army Chaplaincy.* Washington, D.C.: Department of the Army, Office of the Chief of Chaplains, 1977.

Hammond, Jonathan P. *The Army Chaplain's Manual.* Philadelphia: J. B. Lippincott Company, 1863.

Higham, John. *Strangers in the Land.* New York: Atheneum, 1963.

Hofstadter, Richard. *American Political Tradition.* New York: Vintage Books, 1956.

Honeywell, Roy John. *Chaplains of the United States Army.* Washington, D.C.: Department of the Army, Chief of Chaplains, 1958.

Howe, Irving. *World of Our Fathers*. New York: Harcourt Brace Jovanovich, 1976.

Janowsky, Oscar I., Louis Kraft, and Bernard Postal. *Change and Challenge*. New York: National Jewish Welfare Board, 1966.

Jorgensen, Daniel B. *The Service of Chaplains to Army Air Units*. Washington, D.C.: Office of the Air Force Chaplains, 1961.

Karp, Abraham J. *Haven and Home: A History of Jews in America*. New York: Schocken Books, 1985.

Kertzer, Morris N. *With an H on my Dog Tag*. New York: Behrman House, 1947.

Kessner, Thomas. *The Golden Door*. New York: Oxford University Press, 1977.

Kohler, Max J. *Selected Addresses and Papers of Simon Wolf*. Cincinnati: Union of American Hebrew Congregations, 1926.

Korn, Bertram W. *American Jewry and the Civil War*. New York: Atheneum, 1951.

Klein, Isaac. *The Anguish and the Ecstasy of a Jewish Chaplain*. New York: Vantage Press, 1974.

Levinger, Lee J. *A Jewish Chaplain in France*. New York: Macmillan Company, 1921.

Link, Arthur S. *American Epoch*. New York: Alfred A. Knopf, 1956.

Marcus, Jacob R. *Studies of American Jewish History*. Cincinnati: Hebrew Union College Press, 1969.

———. *Early American Jewry*. Philadelphia: Jewish Publication Society of America, 1951.

Marcus, Sheldon. *Father Coughlin*. Boston: Little Brown and Company, 1973.

Margolis, Max J., and Alexander Marx. *A History of the Jewish People*. Philadelphia: Jewish Publication Society of America, 1975.

McPherson, James M. *Battle Cry of Freedom*. Oxford: Oxford University Press, 1988.

Montalto, Nicholas V. *A History of the Intercultural Educational Movement*. New York: Garland Publishers, 1982.

Moore, Deborah D. *At Home in America*. New York: Columbia University Press, 1981.

Mosesson, Gloria. *The Jewish War Veterans Story*. Washington, D.C.: Jewish War Veterans Press, 1971.

Nadich, Judah. *Eisenhower and the Jews*. New York: Twayne Publishers, 1953.

Nave, Orville J. *Nave's Handbook on the Army Chaplaincy*. Los Angeles: Publisher unknown, 1917.

Norton, Herman A. *Struggling for Recognition: The United States Army Chaplaincy.* Washington, D.C.: Office of the Chief of Chaplains, 1971.

O'Brien, David. *American Catholics and Social Reform.* New York: Oxford University Press, 1968.

Poling, Daniel A. *Your Daddy Did Not Die.* New York: Greenberg Publishers, 1944.

Prucha, Francis P. *Broadax and Bayonet.* [Madison]: State Historical Society of Wisconsin, 1953.

Rischin, Moses. *The Promised City.* Cambridge: Harvard University Press, 1962.

Rothenberg, Gunther E. *The Army of Francis Joseph.* West Lafayette, Ind.: Purdue University Press, 1976.

Sachar, Howard M. *The Course of Modern Jewish History.* New York: Random House, 1986.

Shattuck, Gardiner H., Jr. *A Shield and a Hiding Place: The Religious Life of the Civil War Armies.* Macon, Ga.: Mercer University Press, 1987.

Sheerin, John B. *Never Look Back: The Career and Concerns of John J. Burke.* New York: Paulist Press, 1975.

Silbey, Joel H. *A Respectable Minority.* New York: W. W. Norton and Company.

Simpson, George W. *Manual for U.S. Army Chaplains.* Washington, D.C.: War Department, 1893.

Smith, John M. *The Military Ordinariate of the United States,* Washington, D.C.: Catholic University of America, 1966.

Smith, Waldo E. *The Navy and Its Chaplains.* Toronto: Ryerson Press, 1961.

Stover, Earl F. *Up from Handymen: The United States Army Chaplaincy, 1865–1920.* Washington, D.C.: Department of the Army, 1977.

The Torah. Ed. Harry M. Orlinsky. Rev. ed. Philadelphia: Jewish Publication Society of America, 1962.

Thompson, Parker C. *From Its European Antecedents to 1791: The United States Army Chaplaincy.* Washington, D.C.: Government Printing Office, 1950.

Thornton, Francis B. *Sea of Glory: The Magnificent Story of the Four Chaplains.* New York: Prentice-Hall, 1953.

U.S. War Department. *The Chaplain, His Place and Duties: Training Manual.* Washington, D.C.:Government Printing Office, 1926.

U.S. Army. *A Narrative and Factual Report Concerning Chaplain Corps Activities, 1943.* Washington, D.C.: Office of the Army Chief of Chaplains, 1944.

Venzke, Rodger R. *Confidence in Battle—Inspiration in Peace.* Washington, D.C.: Office of the Army Chief of Chaplains, 1977.

Waring, George J. *A Chaplain's Duties and How Best to Accomplish His Work.* Washington, D.C.: Government Printing Office, 1912.

Weigley, Russell Frank. *History of the United States Army.* New York: Macmillan Company, 1967.

Wolf, Simon. *The American Jew as Patriot Soldier and Citizen.* New York: Brentano's, 1895.

Wyman, David A. *The Abandonment of the Jews.* New York: Pantheon Books, 1984.

Young, Mel. *Where They Lie.* New York: University Press of America, 1991.

Zahavy, Zev, ed. *Chaplain on Wings: The Wartime Memoirs of Rabbi Harold H. Gordon.* New York: Sheingold Publishers, 1981.

Zake, Louis J. *The National Department and the Polish American Community, 1919–1923.* New York: Garland Publishing, 1990.

Index

About the Author

Rabbi Albert I. Slomovitz entered the navy the same weekend that he was ordained in June 1979. He has had assignments with navy and marine bases overseas and around the country. One of his most fulfilling tours was as the second Jewish chaplain ever sent to the United States Naval Academy from 1989–1992. He earned his Ph.D. in Ethnic History from Loyola University of Chicago in 1995. Presently, he is Senior Chaplain at the Naval Air Station in Pensacola, Florida. He and his wife, Gail, have four children, Rachel, Aaron, Leah, and Ilana.